LEARN FORWARD

An Invitation To
The Most Important Journeys Of A Child

KARINE VELDHOEN, M.Ed.

Learn Forward Solutions Inc.

PRAISE FOR LEARN FORWARD

"Karine Veldhoen writes with depth and devotion and crafts here a work from an unveiled heart. Learn Forward shines light on our challenge to raise up the next generation, putting words to our unspoken longings and illuminating shaded truths. You'll be confronted, encouraged, and inspired by what could be."

Sean Robinson, Digital Literacy Coach

"What a world this would be if every parent, grandparent, teacher, school administrator would read LEARN FORWARD! Simple, pure and "spot-on" wisdom on child-rearing and student development for all to embrace."

Linda Salata, Principal

"Learn Forward transforms your innermost hopes, dreams, and wishes for your children's success into a tangible framework that serves as a guide for your walk through their most important journeys."

Jennifer Wiebe, Parent & Entrepreneur

"Learn Forward provides a rich starting place for educators and parents to consider their place in a child's journey to literacy, competency, and success. Generous, thoughtful, and honest, this book challenges us to practice courage and become changemakers – personally and professionally."

Dr. Susan Crichton, Director of Faculty of Education

"Learn Forward is your heart in print. The gentle, consistent invitation for all to work together for the good of a child (any child) is the cornerstone of your evident commitment to facilitate the fluency needed to thrive in a world that seems to have settled for merely surviving as the benchmark of success."

Dr. Susannah-Joy Schuilenberg, Psychotherapist

"I cannot think of a more profoundly critical topic; a brilliant embodiment of hope."

Kathryne Sheppard, Leadership Coach

"Learn Forward is a joyous collision of parenting, professional education and leadership. It addresses the desire within us all to "do it well." Learn Forward draws you into communion at the Table of Learning and propels you to act upon the inner longings and deep felt hungers of the human spirit."

Rev. Keith Reisdorf, Senior Pastor

"It is more than a guidebook of what to do, but rather an invitation to a way of living, allowing for personal goals, ideals, and creativity to be welcomed at the Table of Learning."

Janine Draper, Teacher

Published 2015

Learn Forward Solutions, Inc., titles may be purchased in bulk for education,
business, fund-raising or sales promotional use at pricing packaged to share. For
more information, please email hello@learnforward.ca.

In some instances, names, dates, location, and other details have been changed
to protect the identity and privacy of those discussed in this book.

Cover design and illustrations by Roselyn Minnes
Interior design and typesetting by Rich Farr
Artistic direction by Miranda Webb and Karine Veldhoen

Printed in the United States of America

ISBN 978-1-68222-267-6

eBook ISBN

First Edition

Dedicated to my heart's song
David, Daniel, Alyssa, and Gracyn
ilumtli

To all the courageous parents
and educators I've met over the years
who have doubted their sacred work
and wondered whether they are doing a good job.

This book is for you.

CONTENTS

PART FOUR
THE TABLE OF LEARNING

PART FIVE
LEARN FORWARD IN PRACTICE

LEARN FORWARD

changemaking

belonging

selfhood

worthiness

faith

learn forward

YOU'RE INVITED

Mine is the heart of a mother and of a teacher. It throbs with the question, *"How can we Learn Forward together?"*

My relentless search for answers to my driving question is organically evolving from my mothering, classroom, Principal's desk, EdTech, and global humanitarian experiences combined. While I don't have all of the answers, after 20 years and counting I am working with some new insights.

I keep asking. I keep wondering. I cultivate curiosity.

I am certain we must Learn Forward!

I'll never forget the euphoric moments in the summer of 2014 when I sketched out the five most important journeys of a child in my journal. I knew I was at the root of what matters most. The seeds of Learn Forward were taking shape.

Learn Forward is a fresh and hopeful philosophy of learning and human development guiding us to create a more organic learning path for a child; nurturing their growth from the inside out.

The five most important journeys of a child are faith, worthiness, selfhood, belonging, and changemaking. The tree serves as the metaphor.

As a child weaves back and forth, circling and diving deeper into their five journeys, they are growing and developing like a bird close to home. Each journey inextricably linked to the whole.

Learn Forward is about cultivating the conditions for thriving.

In order for children to thrive in the 21st Century, we must change. We must change together. We can only transform the experience of a child, if we gather around the Table as learners.

Knowing we are all learners frees us to iterate, innovate, and correct course. Instead of focusing on getting it right or who got it wrong, we can embrace failure as a stone on a path to mastery.

It is a radical shift in thinking; it is learning-centred. It allows us to courageously pursue our questions and practice designing the conditions for thriving through collaboration, connection, and creativity. There is no finish line. It is a practice worked out in our homes and schools.

We need courage. Courage to embrace the journeys, courage to surrender to the process, courage to dignify each other, courage to believe in the extraordinary potential, and courage to build belonging.

In Part One of Learn Forward, I introduce the hopeful seeds of Learn Forward with three formative stories of courage. In Part Two, I offer a bird's eye view into my personal journey, including my real-life struggle to simplify and get to the heart of what matters most.

Part Three is an exploration of the five journeys through story and lived experiences.

Part Four brings you to the Table of Learning and Part Five provides a series of questions to help you transform the philosophy into practice in your home or school.

You are invited to join me on this journey.

You belong.

You are part of our tribe.

You are welcome.

Let's Learn Forward together!

PART ONE
stories of courage

1

HOLDING SACRED SPACE

We sat as a team of educators and specialists with one mother in an Individualized Education Plan (IEP) meeting at my school, Willowstone Academy.

One mother. Her blonde, Swedish sweetness graced our Table of Learning. She brought the cookies.

Over the course of 90 minutes, we talked about what was a tough year for her son. We documented it in an IEP. Our professional labels and terms floated around the room like elephant balloons. Our language worked to be respectful, but rarely had the generosity we hoped.

Our student, her child, struggled to regulate and stay in school, he could not speak, and related with peers only in the most basic ways. The iPad wasn't helping enough.

We began with strengths. We approach learning from an asset-based paradigm. We developed intentional and personalized learning goals. It was all cordial, reasonable and productive.

Then, at the exhausted end, as the Chief Learning Officer, I asked if we could pause together, with a prayer.

Now, I spent half my career in public schools. I revere the notion of public education. I am a tremendous supporter of the sacred service public educators make to our society. I realize in the context of public education this suggestion would not be in place. But, in my faith-based school, I was permitted.

The permission gave me a window, allowing me to see what matters most.

It was at that moment, holding a sacred space, our truest work unfolded. The tears flowed from our faces as we stood together in a place of surrender. Shoulders shuddered. Maybe it was a tear for the boy who would never speak, maybe the next was for the strain on an overburdened marriage, and maybe some for the faith it took to face each day.

Finally, our tears fell knowing the only place we could stay was at our table in a place of surrender.

Over the years, our work was imperfect. We didn't accomplish enough "functional" goals. We didn't get far enough. The transition to his next school was less than perfect.

However, my memory is crystal clear. I remember being at the Table. A place to pause together and consider what matters most with a silence, softness, and surrender.

2

HER NAME IS PRECIOUS

Have you ever had an experience where there are no easy answers, simple platitudes, or assuaging words? In the crux of the moment, there is only 'being with it,' being with the truth, dignifying the truth, dignifying the human being.

BEING TOGETHER

Niteo Africa is the Canadian charity I started in 2007 to do education projects in East Africa.

The mystery of life is a faith journey for me. My Niteo Africa story began in one of those mysterious moments of faith.

In a tiny corner of Uganda, a little country in sub-Saharan Africa tucked right between Rwanda and the Congo, I visited the village of Rwebisengo.

The trip to the village, as we crawled down onto the Savannah, was hot and dusty, the heat suffocating.

Arriving at the Big Man's house in the village, I found a group of orphans in a *Sound of Music* line up standing in the yard. They lined up to greet ME?!

I had little to offer, but proceeded slowly down the line introducing myself through a translator with pencils and candy in my pocket. The smiles and mutual affection rolled between us on the waves of heat.

When I arrived at the end of the line, I knelt down to meet a girl about age six. I cradled her hand and naively announced,

"Hello, my name is Karine! What's your name?"

I waited, holding the little girl's hand and gaze as my hostess translated for her. The girl shrugged. The question was repeated with a hint of frustration as the girl shrugged her shoulders again. At this moment, there were some nervous giggles from the adults and a couple of the children present.

They have my attention.

They look at me, as I look around and try to sense what is going on.

The girl gazed up at me.

Nervously, my host gripped my shoulder and whispered,

"She doesn't know her name. She doesn't know the name of her family. She is an orphan, and she doesn't know her name."

I rage inside. Who is calling this girl over to them? How does she know where she belongs? How can I fix this?!

Oh! I feel the futility of the pencils and the candy in my pocket! This child who has lost her first teeth has no identity, no name, and no place. She isn't just wearing a stained and torn, pink party dress; she doesn't even have a name!

I look into her eyes, with my own brimming.

With a rush of conviction, connection, and inspiration, I declare with the desperate hope and conviction that one person can change something,

"You are Precious!"

"From now on, and forever, you will be known as Precious!" I proclaim.

What happened at that moment? Was it something profound or simple? Did anything change or move?

A girl's identity began to take shape. Her name echoed through the heavens.

I am comforted and assured because we were together.

Present.
Connected.
Sharing a moment.

We dignified each other's humanity and existence by being together. There was nothing to fix, only two little girls affirming each other. "You are Precious."

Our act of connecting with authenticity called out worthiness and personhood in an act of faith and changemaking.

Years later, I heard through the jungle drums, "She is still called Precious."

3

AM I ENOUGH?

Quite often The Builder, my husband, turns to me with a smile and his resonant baritone voice declares, "We're doin' good."

It always takes my breath away, and it's not because of his grammar.

My body and spirit move profoundly in concert with his encouragement. His words fill my deep hunger.

"We're doin' good."

He speaks to my selfhood. He speaks to my motherhood. He speaks to my sense of belonging.

He reaches out and touches the haunting question, "Am I enough?"

After the school days and the trips to Africa, after I read the bedtime story to my little one and load the dishes from our family-of-five meal, I still relish in the reassurance.

While I realize his reassurance is external, and we all need great self-talk, I think there is something greater at work. We all need to walk together with others and know, "We're doin' good!"

In our homes and schools, can we Learn Forward into the courageous belief of togetherness: we're doin' good?

I wonder if we can learn to walk together, I wonder if we can declare to each other, I wonder if we have the tough tenderness to accept and respect because we truly believe,

'Let's stay together in this place of surrender.'
'You're Precious!'
'We're doin' good!'

My three stories illustrate what matters most. From my experiences as an educator, a humanitarian, a wife and mother, my heart yearns for simplicity. I want to cultivate an artfulness of appreciating the simple things. It takes courage.

Deep in the core of Learn Forward is an invitation. The invitation is to a conversation about the most important journeys of a child.

The most important journeys: faith, worthiness, selfhood, belonging, and changemaking.

Learn Forward is for educators, parents, and leaders who want to courageously invest in the next generation and propel us forward on our path.

I'm holding this space with the hopefulness of reciprocity, our stories weaving together.

I hope in the reading, we will be encouraged to turn to one another and join hands at the Table of Learning: parent, teacher, student, and community. It is a prayer.

Margaret Wheatley reminds us how to join hands,

> *"There is no power greater than a community*
> *discovering what it cares about.*
>
> *Ask 'what's possible?, not what is wrong?' Keep asking.*
> *Notice what you care about.*
>
> *Assume that many others share your dreams.*
> *Be brave enough to start a conversation that matters."*

PART TWO
the path to learn forward

4

MARRIAGE AND MOTHERING

*When jarred by life, we might
unravel the story we tell ourselves
and discover the story we are in,
the one that keeps telling us.*

~ Mark Nepo

I came of age in Southern California, and always knew I wanted to teach. After studying and a year of teaching grade one in the Midwest, I returned. I found myself a young wife and becoming a mother in Orange County.

My children teach me more about teaching than any of my formal degrees. Right from the start, motherhood was a courageous Learn Forward journey.

It began on a steep curve.

My first glimpses of my new son eighteen years ago, as he entered the world, were watching him in the struggle to seize life. It was the breath.

He was struggling to breathe!

In those first minutes of motherhood, his frailty opened up the cavern of my fragility.

What became most important was willing his little heaving body to take in a breath. The minutes of struggle turned into excruciating hours, days, and weeks.

We spent the next five years in intensive early intervention. His courage in taking those first breaths and achieving each milestone from birth to graduating Kindergarten mirrors the journey he is on now as his adulthood dawns. While his cerebral palsy and hearing impairment may slow him down, his pace is just right for brilliance! He inspires me.

My daughter arrived 17 months later, and she is a dynamo! She walked at nine months old and started running at ten! I've been running after her ever since! Her strength, discipline, and intelligence are surpassed only by the sweetness of her laughter. She teaches me about how to be brave in change and bold in life.

Along the path of marriage and mothering, I eventually came to a door called failure. It was dreadful. Eventually, after years of turmoil, I turned the doorknob and walked out.

After our move to Canada, with graduate studies underway, career advancement, and two amazing children, my life collapsed.

While I wish I had walked through that difficult season more gracefully, I struggled with all my might.

I hold my head high knowing I always believed in lifelong love and was learning forward with a new sense of self emerging.

From the pain of divorce, I became a learner. I woke up. I nurtured gratitude. I learned independence. I gained confidence. I stood with faith, thanks to grace. I believed in *lifelong love*, despite my crushing defeat, and *I adored my two children, more than life itself.*

In the rubble of my early thirties, I realized I still had a lot to learn! *Through my salted tears, I began to take blind steps into my future.*

Failure is a stepping stone.

My mother prayed my heart would remain soft.

My school and faith community picked me up and dusted me off. Their hope in me gave me the will to continue. I got up, dressed up, and showed up. Our learning community was and still is a sovereign communion.

5

UNCHARTED TERRITORY

Because I needed to think beyond myself during these major life transitions, I went back to Africa.

I traveled to Africa for the first time when I was 15 and I wanted to go back now as an adult. Travel lit up my curiosity and sense of self. My heart expanded into uncharted territory.

My deepest assumptions were challenged. I met children who had nothing, yet were full of promise.

In Africa, I didn't find a new hierarchy. I found a shared poverty. We were ALL standing with the begging bowl. Healing looked like believing in the potential despite our emptiness. I could see the promise in all things.

Niteo Africa was born. Niteo means, "to bloom, to blossom, to shine, and be bright." It is my wish for African children. It is my wish for all children. It is my wish.

My grass-roots Canadian charity, Niteo Africa, focuses on quality education and aligns perfectly with the work I do in education and with children at Willowstone Academy. It fits together brilliantly.

I hope to cultivate curiosity, creativity, and critical mindedness for all children, all over the world! And, I believe in the dignity of all human beings!

The stories from Africa fill my heart. I have another book full! My brief meeting with Nathaniel captures the work of Niteo best.

When I met Nathaniel, I was simply interviewing students at our second Niteo Africa Literacy Centre at Buunga Hill Primary School. We invited students from every grade to choose their favorite book from the center and come read with us.

Each meeting began with a simple interview.

"What's your name?"
"Nathaniel D."

"How old are you?"
"Nine years old."

"What grade are you in?"
"Grade four."

"Where are you from?"
"South Sudan."

While I knew he wasn't from Uganda, when he answered, my body shuddered, and my skin tingled. I knew South Sudan was boiling with fighting, war, violence, and famine. The turmoil was many years old already.

My mind whirled.

"Nathaniel," I soften, "How long have you been in Uganda?"

"Since 2010," he replies.

He arrived four years earlier.

He came before South Sudan's Independence. He was five. I wondered about his family's safety and continue forward tentatively.

"So, with whom do you live now?" With confidence and ease he replies, "My aunt."

My heart moves in, "Nathaniel when was the last time you saw your mother?"

"In 2010."

At that moment, my motherhood came like a wave from deep in my spirit, welling up through my body.

He hasn't seen his mother in four years! And, without thought or rationale, all I wanted to do was express love to this little guy.

I wanted him to know his mother loves him, and he is precious. I wanted him to know worthiness. I wanted him to know he is safe in Uganda because of the greatest act of love and self-sacrifice a mother could have. I wanted him to have assurance and faith.

I simply said, "Your mother loves you. She loves you very, very much."

As the wars of the world beat down, playing on my heart like mallets on an African drum, Nathaniel opened his books and nonchalantly began to read *Stan the Hot Dog Man*.

He was so proud to read. All he wanted was for me to listen. He read with confidence.

Tears streamed down my face.

Such simple acts of motherhood. Such simple acts of childhood.

Faith bursts forth with worthiness. Selfhood and belonging sing a duet. Changemaking sits in the pages of the book.

While one could interpret this story from many vantage points, I was incredibly moved by Nathaniel's confidence. His mother's love moved me more.

My motherhood whisked in to say something meaningful, an attempt to stand in the gap for mothers around the world who must let go of their children for any reason.

Belonging.
Family.
Story-time.
Imagination.
Connections.
Destiny.

Something in the swirl of these simple acts creates an indescribable energy. My heart stirs. My emotional response is filled with compassion for this child. His brilliant empowerment to 'show off' his reading speaks to me.

Yes, he hasn't seen his mother in four years. For a child Nathaniel's age, it seems like a very long time.

But, what matters most is, he is safe.

Safety allows for a child to journey towards what is most important. It surely doesn't need to look perfect.

Nathaniel's faith comes from the deepest reservoirs of the human spirit. He is confidently becoming his own person. For now, he belongs right where he is. He is changing and growing.

I looked into Nathaniel's soul. The Soul and Self that cannot be named. "It is the being in human being," says Parker Palmer.

He is growing into a unique and vibrant young man. He knows love and belonging. He is getting an education. And, clearly, he values learning!!

On the day I met Nathaniel, he wanted to read *Stan the Hot Dog Man* to me. This simple act of childhood dignified him. Through listening, I was dignified.

At Niteo, we believe that when children read with adults change happens. Imagination unlocks, worthiness settles in, and the work of growing up proceeds with a deep sense of connection.

Everything is so raw in Africa. It is easier to see our humanity. It speaks more clearly to me. And I learn.

I learn about what matters most. I learn about what we need for thriving and what we simply don't. I learn about how to accept the cup of suffering as part of the loving. I learn that we need each other in a deep sense of belonging to move our global village forward.

Niteo Africa gives meaning to the truest and most fundamental aspects of the education process for me! The stories deeply influence Learn Forward.

Education... a meditation on what it means to be human, on knowledge of the self, and our connection to the human community and the natural cosmos.

By Omid Safi

6

THE BUILDER

Several years after my life overhaul and the inception of Niteo Africa, I met The Builder.

He is quiet. He listens. If I am the stormy sea, he is the depth. If I am the wind, he is the anchor.

He adored us. We embraced him. Heaven smiled in redemption.

Bonus baby, number three was born on our ten-month anniversary. Surprise!

My mothering journey stretched out ahead, just as I was rounding the last curve of adolescence with the big kids. I'll be an active, on-duty, mommy for 33 years by the time I'm finished.

Bringing these three children into the world and raising them remains my most underestimated and delightful endeavor to date. It keeps me on my toes to have my heart outside of me wandering on the planet in the form of three lovelies! My three children are my heart's song.

It is from this new vantage point that I am taking a thoughtful look at parenting and education.

I am curious about the role of parents. I am curious about the role of teachers. I hold both in the highest esteem. We are all nurturers.

Between home and school, I can see the barriers and also the bounty. I yearn to cultivate the connection between us. As I imagine the future for children, I am certain we can only achieve transformation, for the sake of the children, together! I call that place the Table of Learning.

My heart yearns to Learn Forward with powerful momentum.

We need to create new cultures of community and mindsets of change, with a focus on the long-term journeys that matter most: faith, worthiness, selfhood, belonging, and changemaking. Focus on these journeys gives us the courage to create thriving!

changemaking

belonging

selfhood

worthiness

faith

learn forward

PART THREE
the five journeys

7

FAITH

Everyone knows firsthand that life is messy and painful, beautiful and unpredictable. The endless practice is keeping our heart open to the whole of it. And the journey of becoming who we were born to be - never ends. It's limitless, eternal. We don't arrive—we grow.

~ Mark Nepo

Rooted in faith, hope, and love. Faith is at the heart of all things.

I see it in my journey as a woman and mother. It is a deep current throughout all my work with children in Africa and North America. The theme of faith permeates the fabric of our lives.

What does faith mean to a child? How do they capture it? Could it be essential? What does faith mean to me?

FALLING INTO FAITH

My life doesn't present as 'needy.' And yet, I know deep spiritual hunger.

As I look back on the story of my life, I find a simple truth:

When I fall, I fall into faith.

Bruised and broken, I have a portfolio of failure; noise and confusion mixed with trauma and rebellion.

If you saw the movie of my life, you definitely would see it: a montage of messiness. Personally, I don't do anything without a good dose of a fight.

But, faith is always there. Knit into my life since childhood.

FAITH is an experience of:

Comfort.

*A wholehearted trust
in the restoration of all things.*

A whispered invitation of hopefulness.

A beckoning to the dance of life!

I have the privilege of being called "mother" by three children. At the time of this writing, they are two teens and a tot. One calls me "mother," one says "mummy," and sometimes I get "mom" too! Even that could change tomorrow.

I am an, 'in practice' mom.

In many ways these three vibrant youngsters are leading me, and I am simply trying to keep up!

I had a significant emotional reaction (the ugly cry) the first time I heard Natalie Grant's song, "When I Leave The Room." My tears streamed thinking about how the powerful lullaby lyrics related to my parenting journey.

Besides chronicling the remarkable mommy journey I'm on, seemingly in every stage simultaneously, the song takes me to a scary, almost dreadful place when she sings,

"There's nothing more that I can do..."

I don't know about you, but I'm always doing something. I have an inexhaustible belief in asking, *"What is the next right thing to do?"*

I am a student of soul work, but I'm an expert at being busy.

And in the most frightening moments, I get to the end of doing.

There is nothing more that I can do.

As Chief Learning Officer of a school, I listen to the parenting hearts around me. I can see them pounding fists in those dreadful places: illness, disability, defiance, distance, exhaustion, waiting, and confusion. I think every parent knows this dark corner.

What happens when I back into it?

Again, I have to confess, I am a fighter. I wish my mommy instincts looked more graceful than primal. But, I'm on a learning journey.

I see recurring primal instincts surface frequently in my office as well. We all experience fight-flight-freeze reactions as we watch our children struggle for any reason.

We all have instincts for our children. Survival instincts.

And, sometimes there is nothing more I can do. *What happens then?*

After I've fought with school, parents, my child, my spouse, and myself, it doesn't help. My heart is completely shredded and incapacitated.

What happens when there is nothing more I can do?

I remember... There's nothing more I can do, but just fall more in love with you!

...but "just fall more in love with you!"

A place of love. A place of faith.

Stroking her hair as she falls asleep, championing his courage to face another day, kissing her on the cheek to say, "I'm proud of you." A safe place.

A gentle place of acceptance. The sacred work of my soul softens reactive survival instincts.

With a soft heart, we can take a long-term perspective of faith. We can trust God to hold us all. It isn't rushed. There is peace. There is surrender.

With a soft heart, we can allow our tears, engage with others from a place of vulnerability, acknowledge our fears, and support our children to find their place.

Really, at the end of the day, it's about "falling more in love with you."

With a soft heart and sincere courage, we can give our children what they want most from us, our compassionate, present attention.

With a soft heart, we can let go and trust.

With faith,

Waves of love crash over me and a steady current of calm flows through my heart.

I am inspired to be better.

Breathe intentionally.
Dig deeper.
Open more.
To trust.

I have a meaningful purpose.

I realize my breath today has a reason for being. I take simple steps to walk into my purpose. My reason for being is greater than I am.

I am a changemaker. Changemakers are changed.

I find the courage and grace to enter softly into a new day.

I fall into faith.

FAITH TRANSFORMS

I saw the simple transformation of faith in full color when I cared for baby Kate over several weeks on a Niteo trip. I learned that faith changes what is unhealthy into what is full of life!

It was 2009 and The Builder had just entered our lives. Love was in the air.

When I traveled to Africa that July, I cared for Kate in an orphanage called "Joy."

Kate's little life is a perfect forever-picture of transformation.

Vulnerable. Abandoned. Dying.
Becomes
Worthy. Lovely. Chosen.

When I met Kate, she was almost a year old and 11 lbs. She lay unresponsive in a crib in a bleak orphanage in East Africa. Her mother couldn't care for her and had abandoned her in the community toilet. She was a very sick little girl.

The sight in the orphanage was indescribable. Her condition and the environment offered little hope. Survival a dim light on the horizon.

My own soul knows those places. The deserted and rejected places. My awareness of those abandoned and barren places gnaws away at my heavy heart.

The typical one-year developmental milestones were only a dream for Kate. She wasn't eating. She wasn't crying. She was dehydrated. Her skin sagged dry and thin like rice paper. Our team nurse, from Canada, looked at me and said, "It's not good."

Our team's mothering instincts ran thick for Kate. Faith abounded. Prayers went forth. We researched and consulted, but more than that we rocked, and we nourished.

"Every child worthy," sang faithfully in our hearts. "Every child..."

Over the weeks we visited, Kate transformed. She began to suckle. Her skin took some shape. She started to look around. Her big beautiful eyes opened and started following us. She miraculously even lifted her head. She raised her head! Her simple gesture of strength became a new song in our hearts.

Kate went on to regain strength and eventually a loving family in Uganda adopted her. We know we were a small part of her journey.

I think the Universe allowed me to bear witness to Kate's transformation in 14 days, holding a place of faith because faith is how we stand through the journey. Faith transforms.

There is always a whispered invitation of hopefulness.

Schools and homes, parents and teachers cannot transform. It is our faith that transforms. It is our belief.

Faith holds the remarkable hope that all things are sacred. With the gentlest of hands, faith believes that ultimately all things are restored. We don't have to be afraid.

FAITH IS BELIEF

In *The Power of Habit*, Charles Duhigg writes about the research UC Berkeley, Brown University, and the National Institute of Health began to do on the effectiveness of Alcoholics Anonymous.

They found, "It was belief itself that made a difference. Once people learned how to believe in something, that skill started spilling over to other parts of their lives until they started believing they could change. Belief was the ingredient that made a reworked habit loop into a permanent behavior."

The power comes from faith.

While, for Kate, her belief was not yet formed, our faith carried her. For many of the older children I know, faith transforms their confidence and sense of self.

Recently, I was speaking at a school assembly with my whole student body on this concept of transformation. We had the egg and chick, the caterpillar and butterfly. And, we had Johnny.

Now during the assemblies I have with my students, I always like to engage them. It is truly my big classroom. They love it because they get to speak into the microphone. It is a good understanding.

But, during my presentation on transformation, I asked,

"How does spiritual transformation happen within us?"

I know, I know! It is a terribly abstract and challenging concept. Sometimes, I think children have a deeper wisdom than we give them credit.

Then, Johnny. He doesn't just raise his hand; he raises it with a smirk. Oh dear.

Johnny is a student who sits with his math whiteboard drawing Homer Simpson. He is small and feisty. He is bright and capable. His cheeks and dimples are to die for, and our goal is to channel his boundless energy.

I am wise enough these days to see the potential; putting a microphone in front of Johnny's mouth, in front of the student and parent community, could spell disaster.

What can I say, I like risk.

I prompted with a prayer,

"Johnny what is your best thinking answer? How does spiritual transformation happen in us?"

To my delight, Johnny confidently responded,

"Spiritual transformation is about moving from normal to extraordinary!"

Eureka! Chills!

*Being,
becoming
and
believing
is the
signature of process.*

It is deep at the roots, where children learn to believe.

More than teaching children to achieve, we must teach them to believe! We can teach them, through powerful metaphors, poetry, stories of faith, and modeling. Johnny knows a secret of the universe and, by the way, he shared it brilliantly!

You are also carried on the expansive and mighty wings of belief into the transformative power of worthiness, selfhood, belonging, and changemaking.

We teach.
We learn.
It is a paradox.

FAITH IS OUR COURAGE FOR BELONGING

We are haunted: war, abuse, slavery, conflict, and tragedy of every kind. It inundates from every source of connectedness, ironically terrorizing us with how divided and how conquered we are. It is an ugly face. We shudder.

It takes courage to stand in the tender gap between what is and what could be.

It takes courage to believe in community when humanity is so oriented to grab, fight, and defend.

The answers are deeper.

The responses are courageous and full of a Greater Grace.

True faith binds us together. It beckons us to the dance of life.

Let's talk more about that when we get to Belonging. For now, just know faith binds us together in a process called: Learn Forward.

Knowing that faith is foundational for a child helps us intentionally weave faith work into our interactions. The faith that guides and nourishes us is contagious. It allows us to believe, it allows us to belong, it allows us to transform. When we move from a faithful place, one of courage and hope, we Learn Forward.

8

WORTHINESS

Once we believe in ourselves we can risk curiosity,
wonder, spontaneous delight, or any experience
that reveals the human spirit.

~ E. E. Cummings

WORTHINESS IS SACRED SOUL WORK

Laura Hillenbrand explores the idea of resilience through unfathomable torture and hardships in her book *Unbroken: A World War II Story of Survival, Resilience, and Redemption*. I am so surprised by where she gets to in her exploration of how resilience connects with a sense of worthiness. She writes,

> ...the guards sought to deprive them of something that had sustained them even as all else had been lost: dignity. This self-respect and sense of self-worth, the innermost armament of the

soul, lives at the heart of humanness; to be deprived of it is to be dehumanized, to be cleaved from, and cast below, mankind... without dignity, identity is erased. In its absence men are defined not by themselves, but by their...circumstances.

Forming the innermost armament of the soul, worthiness, is sacred soul work.

The problem is: I'm not always sure how that happens. It ebbs and flows. I can't put my finger on it. There isn't a great formula or recipe for worthiness.

At that point, honestly, I look at the patterns in my life.

The truth is, my sense of worthiness is scrapped together like a patchwork quilt.

It is being formed on the potter's wheel of 'trying to overcome' and 'fired in the heartbreaks of life.' Understanding my own worthiness is my sacred, soul work.

Throughout, I can see some patterns emerging that are helpful and hopeful.

WORTHINESS IS OVERCOMING

How can we model a sense of worthiness for our children?

Have you ever been more defined by your circumstances than by your sense of self? I have.

Have you ever struggled to know you are worthy without having to win, be the best, work the hardest, or perform? I have.

You see, I think we try too hard because if we don't, then we can't find a sense of worthiness! So, we run on our hamster wheel hoping to create a solid inner reality.

Shame and worthiness expert Brené Brown explains, it is the exact opposite of working for our worthiness. Her research shows worthiness comes from being vulnerable enough to embrace our imperfections. It isn't a constant state of worthiness, but rather a process to practice.

Worthiness flows from the practice of overcoming our fear of vulnerability.

It's a relief to me.

I originally conceived of worthiness as soaring, but maybe it is more like waddling, on the inside.

So, when difficult things happen, we must speak to ourselves about our value and our imperfections with compassion.

Children need infinite amounts of practice with this process.

School and home must link arms to reinforce a culture of worthiness in children. We must be like-minded in our focus on the value, beauty, and potential of each child, which transcends the report card, MVP awards, or medals around their neck.

As we practice together, we are released into more joy, abundance, and love.

For our family, I can see that release when we can dance to "Kiss the Girl" by Keith Urban in the kitchen while simply frosting our cookies! We can find happiness.

Resilience and overcoming looks like cultivating compassion and worthiness in the little moments!

WORTHINESS HOLDS A CHILD

We adore following our high school daughter's athletics. We followed a recent provincial volleyball tournament via text. She was far away. We had commitments and couldn't go. We sent our hearts with her and texted.

Each game she would text us the results and her intentions for the next game.

The rhythm was warm and responsible. Our connection was weak, but real. The team fought through. Her game-by-game intentions showed maturity. She played hard. It was an emotional weekend for her. I could tell.

At the end of her weekend, she asked if we could connect via FaceTime.

Of course! She wanted to talk! The call came.

When she called, my heart was fully open to her. I couldn't wait to hear from her! There wasn't an ounce of hesitation. Talking, connecting, spending time; yes, those are my love languages!

Drop everything. Listen open-heartedly. Be present.

At the end of the day, I think she needed to hear, "I love you! You're wonderful! We're with you. It's okay."

As the words echo, they are the words we all need to hear. My heart aches to hear those words as I lay my head on the pillow at day's end.

I love you! You're wonderful! We're with you! It's okay!

We all need to hear words of acceptance, companionship, and worthiness.

We need to hear these words to bolster our hearts with courage. We need courage for the next day.

Some of us get those words from a loved one. If we do, those words echo in the heavens. What a blessing!

But the haunting reality is, our human relationships are fragile. We seem to know deep down, ultimately, those words need to come from the whisper inside us.

On some level, we all need to believe in ourselves.

The truth is, each of us has to navigate different crises throughout life when the only believable source of worthiness is the spiritual truth inside.

We must learn it from the inside out.

WORTHINESS FLOWS FROM FAITH

What is the shape of worthiness?

Not only is it a practice, but it is an inner journey, a spiritual journey.

It is a spiritual journey that takes us into the depths.

A waddle versus a soaring, a journey for the courageous: a sense of worthiness develops as we embrace our vulnerabilities.

How can we face the shadow? How can we look at our shame? How can a child face failure and overcome? How can he see what is 'disabled' in him? How can she heal her hurts? How can we survive the anxieties that threaten our existence?

As human beings, we have such deep-rooted need. How can we find worthiness?

The continuation of the story of Louis Zamperini in *Unbroken* ends with him coming to the brink of breaking. After an unimaginably shameful and physically wrenching captivity in Japan during WWII, Zamperini is physically rescued and returns to the U.S. However, his soul is not free.

Healing doesn't come effortlessly or quickly.

Zamperini becomes a drunk, continues to be tortured by his tormentors in nightmares, and begins to plot murderous revenge in his mind. While the physical experience of captivity is over, his very being remains toxic.

It was a further descent.

When Zamperini arrived in the depths, there wasn't a dungeon waiting, it was faith. The story culminates with Zamperini's spiritual experience of grace.

When mercy kisses our souls, we find freedom, healing, and wholeness.

Like Zamperini's profound experiences, our greatest gifts are fashioned by our downward descents, our inner journeys to humble places, where the only option is to embrace our vulnerabilities.

When we get there, our spirit can find grace.

We can find Heaven's kiss.

We can find a new assurance.

If we know the great gifts are in the struggle, why are we so afraid when we see difficulties happening for our children?

Resilience, grit, and perseverance develop in challenging and gut-wrenching places. As parents and educators, we have to support, love, and come alongside children. However, they aren't served when we save, panic, rescue, or flee.

Our best gift is a practice of courage: a gentle compassion towards all that is unfinished.

O trust me, as a mother, I do not always feel a gentle compassion. But, when I do it works better.

What I know for sure is there is a love greater than mine. It helps me. The heavens open and I can rest.

As Parker Palmer writes in *Let Your Life Speak*, "Grace flows from the deep knowledge that identity depends only on the simple fact that we are children of God, valued in and for ourselves."

Faith and worthiness, of the truest forms, are inextricably linked.

PRACTICE WORTHINESS IN FAILURE

Every mother wants her child to achieve. Every father wants to know his child is a winner!

However, what do we do when our child competes and doesn't win? What do we do when our child doesn't end up at the top? What happens, when in comparison, our child doesn't compare?

What does worthiness whisper in those moments when the world says, "You don't measure up!"

How can we reframe success to ensure all children accept failure as a stone on a path to mastery?

Over the past four years, my son competed in debate. Recently, I attended the British Columbia Debate Provincial Tournament at the prestigious St. George's School in Vancouver, sponsored by the Law Foundation Cup.

My grade twelve son competed amongst 160 debaters, with 70 senior debaters. In 20 hours, each pair would debate five times: two prepared debates and three impromptu debates. The context was infused with the grandest of expectations, and the students' swagger made me sweat.

What you have to know about this story are three things:

- My son competes with cerebral palsy and a moderate-severe hearing impairment

- He's been competing in debate since Grade 9.

- In his first Provincial debate in Grade 9, he finished dead last: sixtieth out of sixty. As he reflects on that experience, he confesses, "And, I cried like a baby."

By the world's standards, he lost. He came in last.

But, he kept going.

This year, we were aiming for the top two-thirds. I reflected with him about his journey at the end of the weekend, before the results were released.

I asked him, "How did you make it to Grade 12 Provincials? How did you overcome? How did you continue forward under such immense pressure and with such enormous obstacles to overcome? How did you climb that mountain of pursuit?"

He graciously replied, "Mother, I don't ever compete for the sake of achievement or accolade because that would be unhealthy. I always just run the race against myself."

You know, I could write pages and pages about worthiness and I likely still will, but really, my son says it all:

"I don't ever compete for the sake of achievement or accolade because that would be unhealthy. I always just run the race against myself."

While I think many practices cultivate worthiness in our children, I believe we need these simple reminders.

At my school, the way Coach Wiebe says it is,

"Cheer for the swing!"

I call it: Learn Forward.

True faith offers us a sense of worthiness. Worthiness helps us rise above failure, trauma, and shame. We can accept others and ourselves; along with all that is unfinished. Worthiness is one of the most important journeys of a child and helps us Learn Forward.

9

SELFHOOD

...God creates things that create themselves.
Wouldn't this be the greatest way that God could create --
to give autonomy, freedom, and grace to things to keep
self-creating even further?

~ Richard Rohr

At Willowstone Academy, we penned the words "...climbing to the peaks of selfhood and belonging..." in our school manifesto. The phrase is worthy of unpacking as a spiritual and developmental journey of a child.

Let's begin with selfhood.

In some ways, our culture supports the journey of selfhood more effectively and holds it as a higher priority. We are intentional about the needs of the individual and consider it a higher value than the needs of the group.

I love Back-to-School Night at the beginning of the school year, because it is the first time to come together as a big community of parents, teachers, and students. It's a traditional event when parents and teachers gather to learn about our year together.

The burning question on every parent's mind is, "How will you meet the needs of my child?"

The question is a priority for every parent and educator throughout the school year.

The faculty at our school understands how important discussing this question is. We discuss personalization, individualization, and differentiation with ardor. We want each child's needs to be met.

We know every child is unique. We want to celebrate every child's uniqueness!

Intuitively, as parents and teachers, we are aware of how important it is to nurture each child's sense of identity. Their distinctive qualities, driving motivations, and passions, as well as their weaknesses, must be knit together throughout childhood.

The question percolates, "What is the journey of selfhood?"

SELFHOOD EMERGES IN SECURITY

Each child deserves to thrive as an individual. Each child must form and discover who they are! Our schools and homes need to be safe enough for this journey.

Dr. Seuss agrees. In his light-hearted five lessons of life, he proclaims:

1. Today you are You, that is truer than true. There is no one alive who is Youer than You.

2. Why fit in when you were born to stand out?

3. You have brains in your head. You have feet in your shoes. You can steer yourself any direction you choose.

4. Be who you are and say what you feel, because those who mind don't matter and those who matter don't mind.

5. Today I shall behave as if this is the day I will be remembered.

Along with Dr. Seuss, the research of Dr. Gordon Neufeld among many others also supports the notion of the child's emerging individuality.

Dr. Neufeld, the author of *Hold On To Your Kids*, discusses the developmental stage as emergence. We can see it begin at age two and then again powerfully in the teen years when the drive for independence is strongest.

I had two teens and a two-year-old all at the same time.

Yes, you can laugh now!

It was a lesson in how little control I have. My kind husband, The Builder, whispered reminders in my ear like, "Let her decide," and "He'll figure it out."

Even though I don't always welcome his words, he reminds me about what matters most. Talk about requiring courage!

Everything, with all three children, had to be conversational and dignifying.

Emergence described by Dr. Neufeld looks like:

- A vitality (not easily bored)
- A sense of agency and initiative
- Viability as a separate being
- Full of interests and curiosities
- A relationship with self
- A strong quest for independence

> *For children, emergence comes within the context of secure and safe relationships. The vital connections of nurturer-child provide the foundation from which children grow and then launch with a true sense of self.*

When did your sense of self begin to emerge? How?

I agree with Richard Rohr, about the climb to selfhood, "…I haven't met a life yet that's a clear and straight line to a truth, to self, or to God."

What is incredible is witnessing, supporting, and occasionally providing handholds on the journey of a child's self-discovery!

At the end of Back-to-School Night, our Grade 2 teacher and I were debriefing about how it went. She said, "I told the parents I am crazy about their kids, and I think they knew I meant it. It made them feel good."

Children need us to be 'crazy' about them! Weaving messages of love and acceptance into the journey gives children the courage to take new ground!

THRIVING IS AT THE CENTRE OF SELFHOOD

My extended family is magnetically drawn to one another! At one point last summer I had seven teenagers from my family asleep in my home! What a joy!

They played hard during the day: beach volleyball, stand-up paddle-boarding, golfing, swimming, and bouncing on the big blob in the lake. I love summer!

With seven teenagers, there is a boatload of emergent energy around the questions of "Who am I?" and "Who am I becoming?"

As we watched them play and chatted, we could see them sitting with those questions. We were mindful of them.

As I consider children, I am again amazed at the extraordinary potential that lives within every child.

The "extraordinary potential within every child" inspires me to consider how we can support them as individuals.

It is so much less about where the children are going to school or what classes they are enrolled. In my case, the seven students attended seven different schools between Grades 7-12.

It is more about their attitudes and engagement on the learning journey.

The Table of Learning is a feast!

How can we best support lifelong success?

To answer that question, I came across a research question by Dr. Sabre Cherkowski, "What if we imagine that the primary role of teachers is to learn how to thrive as educators, and, in so doing, to continually co-explore and facilitate all means by which everyone in their learning communities thrives most of the time?"

Let's just replace "teachers" and "learning communities" with "parents" and "homes."

"What if we imagine that the primary role of parents is to learn how to thrive as humans, and, in so doing, to continually co-explore and facilitate all means by which everyone in their home thrives most of the time?"

What if the central question for teachers and parents is: how do we thrive? What if we need to thrive as individuals for the sake of our children?

I went all over Uganda, Africa, last summer encouraging,

"Let's move from surviving to thriving!"

If we are all learners, aiming for thriving, it sets the tone for children!

The seven teenagers in my home also need to consider,

"What is thriving? For me?"

Let me give you a personal example. For me, thriving means letting go of the lifelong notion of "I am not an athlete." As a teenager, I was too busy practicing the piano to play volleyball.

However, today thriving looks like adopting a new self-perception; thriving today is learning.

Now, I need to move my body. I need to embrace that I can swim, run, bend, and play! I need to embrace a new aspect of myself to thrive! When I do, the seven teenagers in my house will benefit. My learning community will benefit.

Dare I say we will create a better humanity?

I am not advocating for a narcissistic, egocentric, or self-indulgent model. We must consider health and well-being for ourselves as individuals.

We must model thriving.

It must be considered. We must dig deep and ask powerful questions about what thriving looks like for us as parents, as teachers, and for our children.

And, we must consider what thriving looks like before we race into scheduling ballet, soccer, and French lessons in a selfless and driving hurry.

SELFHOOD EMERGES THROUGH DREAMING

As a child, I believed in wishes and fairies and birthday candles.
Belief rolled into faith in bigger things. But, something deeply
significant lives inside a child's imagination, meaning-making and
dreaming.

It's personal.
It's unique.

Education is wrestling with how to personalize learning. We are
considering time, pacing, and place. Teachers offer "choice" and
ensure experiences are designed to be right at the edge of each
child's learning. We collaboratively write goals with students
and parents. At every turn, we adapt for students who need
something different.

But, this week the description of our Grade 1 teacher's leaf art
challenged me. She relayed how children could look at a leaf and
"see" an animal, all sorts of creatures, with eyes and arms and
stripes! Young children are describing in detail what they see in
their imaginations, not just one child, almost all of them!

Only moments earlier our teaching team read this quote together
by Erwin McManus in *The Artisan Soul*,

> "...only in our imagination can we accomplish anything, go
> anywhere, or become anyone; only in our imagination do we
> have boundless possibilities and endless potential; only in our
> imagination can we even begin to conceive of what reality might
> become if it began to reflect the imagination of God."

And then...

I had this thought...

What if the greatest gift we can give a child, the most personalized learning experience is one that unlocks imagination?

What if the height of personalizing learning is unlocking a child's imagination?

What if, metaphorically, we can only achieve our potential if we can see the elephant in the fall leaf!

What if we need to dream?

In our home, we place a high value on imagination!

Each year the Builder and I set aside a whole weekend to dream with each other! We call it our visioning weekend!

Learn Forward is calling us to build imagining into our ethos and celebrate children who can 'see' with eyes of faith.

When dreams unlock an individual's selfhood, we call it:
Learn Forward.

INDEPENDENCE ENCOURAGES SELFHOOD

Educators are key in setting high expectations for children to be independent.

Parents must also support children in their journey towards selfhood by infusing life with an expectation of independence. It's the notion of,

"I will always encourage my child towards independence!"

As a mother, each year I ask how I need to support my child to greater independence. It might be lunches or dorm rooms, dishes or reading.

Ensuring our children gain independent life skills is essential to the development of selfhood.

My parents always say it is easier to learn to parent than to learn to de-parent. They're right. Standing back and allowing for greater independence is a definite challenge.

As I enter into the final year of active parenting with my oldest, I'm deeply considering his independence, his readiness and confidence to take on responsibility. For him, I am thinking about more specific budgeting practices, independent living skills, and study routines for university.

For the littlest one, well, she is three, and she needs to learn to manage her backpack, snacks, and water bottle for preschool. Routines support success for each new skill.

A great place for families to begin routine independence training is with homework. Homework can be a real school-days battleground. Right from the start, parents can help make homework the child's responsibility. I don't mean right from the start of the year, I mean right from the start of your child's school days.

With one BIG caveat, children need parents to hold them accountable to do it!

They may not be entirely intrinsically motivated to get their work done. None of us is always intrinsically motivated. So, children need to know you are checking in with both your child and their teacher in some form. They may need support getting started and checking in at the end.

Encourage their strengths and support their challenges like the scaffolding circling a new building.

We need to believe in their extraordinary potential!

Homework will be easier if we are at the Table of Learning with the teacher.

Open and heart-full conversations can happen at the Table.

Supporting homework success is easy! In a family meeting, ask your child what support he or she might need from you to complete homework independently. Build a routine you all agree upon in advance. Ensure the right supplies and space are set-up.

Don't expect perfection. Be ready to 'let things go' sometimes. Homework is the child's work.

This big picture work of moving children towards independence is the work of parents supporting the journey of selfhood. My heart guides me on this hike. I mindfully consider what my child is currently doing and build from there. Start with baby steps.

While it may be easier to keep doing things for my children, it doesn't serve them. Besides, nothing makes little ones feel more capable than successfully taking on new responsibilities.

We Learn Forward.

Selfhood is developed when we all pursue thriving; when we model it. Dreams are at the centre of selfhood, with personal responsibility around the edges, and secure relationships forming the bedrock. Then, children can 'be themselves' with confidence.

10

BELONGING

Because true belonging only happens when we present our authentic, imperfect selves to the world, our sense of belonging can never be greater than our level of self-acceptance.

~ Brené Brown, Gifts of Imperfection

The Learn Forward model holds the journey of selfhood in balance with the journey of belonging.

Belonging represents the journey of creating meaningful relationships.

Complex social-emotional competencies such as empathy, effective communication, and problem solving must develop to equip children for this journey. Belonging must be practiced within community and relationships for the competencies to develop over time.

How can we understand this journey further? How can we practice and model the creation of meaningful relationships? What handholds can we find on the climb to belonging?

BELONGING IS HEART-SHAPED

Belonging is a huge developmental concept that doesn't come with a 'how-to' manual to help us deepen our understanding. We need to understand it in our hearts.

I think the consummate experience of a child's sense of belonging is when the door creaks at three o'clock in the morning and I hear the pad-pad of a 3-year old little girl's feet down the hall. She's had a dream. She stands at my bedside, and I pull her into me. I whisper,

"You can have some cozy cuddles before you go back to bed."

She presses her littleness into my comfort. I smell the baby shampoo from last night as my chin rests on her head. She belongs in my arms. She knows she belongs. The blanket of sleep comes easily now.

Children belong in our care.

From there, we explore another concept. It is the concept of community:

A learning community,

A school.

How do we belong to each other in a community?

When we step back from the why and how of education and the selfhood journey, we can see what it means to belong to a community. We can see how each person in relationship with

others must give up some level of autonomy and individuality to build a community that extends beyond selfhood.

We have to expend time and energy. We have to 'let go' of some things in order to gain something greater.

On a team, you must wear a uniform. In a classroom, you must be respectful. In community organizations, you must follow the path designed for volunteers. While these 'rules' may hamper our individuality, they give us something greater: belonging.

While I realize one should never give up personhood to be in relationships with another, there is a dance between selfhood and belonging. They must be in balance.

Belonging will ask us to empathize, realize we can't control everything, face disappointment, learn from others and be touched by their hurts and joys.

It is right there, in the tapestry of faith, at the heart of being together, where compassion and changemaking are born.

How do 5-year-olds understand belonging? Well, sometimes they are better at it than we are and sometimes they're not great at it yet.

With their parents, children tend to feel a deep sense of belonging, but on the playground, they may hit someone else with a willow tree branch on the head. That's normal. So, we communicate, coach, and care. Growth happens.

Children at every stage are thinking about both independence (selfhood) and friendship (belonging). There are anchor charts in classrooms all over North America to prove this.

When we're at school, it can be challenging because sometimes other children are going through difficult seasons, and they show us their pain or incapacity to cope in inappropriate ways. Our knee-jerk reaction: we want to create space. It is too difficult. I feel it too. Of course, we want to shelter our child.

The greater good is to reach toward it.
Surround that pain with support.

It isn't easy. People are hurt, frustrated, and wired for vengeance.

So, while we are all learning to respect people's hearts, property, and space, let's remember that each child is developing differently. They are little. They are learning.

I've never met a child who at his or her core didn't want to fit in, who didn't want to belong, who didn't want to do the right thing.

Research tells us that the number one indicator of happiness is meaningful relationships with others. In our hearts, everyone wants to belong.

> *There can be no vulnerability without risk. There can be no community without vulnerability. There can be no peace, and ultimately no life, without community.*
>
> ~M. Scott Peck

BEING TOGETHER CREATES PEACE

What if little girls and little boys around the world connected and slept with each other's toys? What affection, what tenderness, and what grace would we achieve?

My girlfriend asked me about the story-telling evening organized with Okello Kelo Sam. My friend, Okello, was sharing his experiences as a former child soldier in Uganda. She wondered if it was appropriate for her 8-year-old daughter to attend with her. She imagined the details of his story were likely horrifying.

I asked her,

"How does your daughter sleep? Does she frighten easily?"

But life has funny ways of teaching me such wondrous lessons! I'm always on this Learn Forward journey! I learn lessons of softening, opening, connecting, without fear. I'm humbled.

Okello is my friend. He is my brother. He is wise beyond words. He connects authentically with everyone he meets without pretense. He is a man who at any given time carries the weight of providing for and educating over 250 victims of war at Hope North in Northern Uganda, with over 3000 rescued in total. He leads Hope North with an effervescent lightness and joy that is unquenchable!

What happened next in our story is simply sensational!

My girlfriend brought her daughter to see Okello speak. The little innocent connected with Africa with eagerness. She drank up sameness across continents, generations, and incomparable life experiences. She viscerally knew the kindness and warmth that Okello shares in his smile. Purpose achieved.

A global citizen, a changemaker was born in the joyful connection!

Her heart so stirred with the dreaminess of childhood, she hummed and drummed herself to sleep with her body wrapped around Okello's cowhide drum like a hand around a peach.

A joyful connection means,

I will sleep with my African drum made in Northern Uganda.

Belonging exists when we wrap our arms around humanity, accept and cherish with abandon, and delight in the rhythm of life. When learning goes beyond the classroom and into the world, it is a peaceful connection of belonging!

BELONGING IS COURAGEOUS

I wrote about the season of back-to-school in the selfhood chapter, but it also is illustrative for belonging.

Going back to school is the quintessential journey of selfhood and belonging. Every human being wants to be unique and valued while also fitting in and creating meaningful friendships. On the first day of school, every child sits in the tension of these two branches of 'becoming' and it is a big deal! Worthiness is being shaped.

Back-to-School butterflies are normal. Everyone feels a certain amount of fear. How we cope with fears shapes a lifetime of success.

I'll never forget my daughter's first day of high school. She's dressed and ready to go with her backpack and her new clothes. Acceptance and belonging were clearly a high priority. I wished her well, happy we could share the experience.

When she returned home and I asked her how it went, she told me about how between classes, in the busy hallway, she fell!

Now, this is my coordinated, athletic child. She fell in the hallway. On the first day! O, dear! My heart sank!

Then, something remarkable happened. She added,

"But, I just laughed and everyone else laughed with me. It happens to everyone, Mom."

All I could do is look at her and say,

"I'm so proud of you!"

I'm pretty sure I would not have handled it that well. In fact, I can remember the shame of falling in the Grade 8 hallway and it still burns in my throat. We are all trying so hard to fit in with others.

It is at school when children must exercise their courageous belonging muscles to make new friends, adjust to changes, overcome challenges, and learn to believe in themselves in the process.

The journey to selfhood is treacherous, and the testing ground is in belonging.

Do I fit in at school?
Do I have friends I trust?
Am I creating meaningful relationships?

Our deepest fears revealed, "If I cannot be loved for who I am, then who I am might be fatally flawed." We all have that fear and we can see it haunt children.

Children are working hard to 'figure out who they are' and ensure they 'fit in.' They are practicing. In my experience, the pressure seems to begin heightening around Grade 4 and continues to pick up pace throughout puberty.

All of the sudden they won't participate in a previous passion because it might not be cool. They misbehave at home because they feel under pressure at school. They withdraw, and you can't understand why they don't want to spend time with you. Sleep time becomes a battleground because children are bravely stepping out in new ways. Or maybe they are in the car with you, and as you pull into the driveway, they drop their head into their hands and sob.

Ask me how I know. It has all happened to me, maybe even in one week!

What they need most to protect their hearts during those times is at least one adult who is 'crazy about them!' If there are more, even better!

Parents and teachers can work together to let kids know they are safe. When we work together our courage and commitment are bolstered. It takes time, patience, and a deep faith that it will work out.

Weaving in and out of the journeys: faith, worthiness, selfhood, belonging, and changemaking.

Of course, sometimes children aren't safe in a community. I don't mean someone called them a name or they feel left out on the playground. I'm talking about the potential danger at the hands of a powerful and relentless peer group.

As parents and teachers, the reality weighs like a heavy stone on our hearts, the tragedy like an unspeakable darkness.

Belonging calls us to gather near, listen deeply, ask open and honest questions, so our hearts are softened, and we can create a new hope together.

How can we court our children into the safety of our arms? How can we give a child the message, "I'm crazy about you!" in a way that's meaningful to them? Let's celebrate the new and renewed courage to create meaningful relationships of belonging!

"Entwined with Humanity" Means Team

Our school manifesto includes the words "entwined with humanity." We practice belonging to each other in a community through a gentle acknowledgment of how we are all connected.

Once, on my way to dropping my daughter off at her summer job at the ice cream shop, she told me about her fall volleyball team. Her coach's strategy was to create a cohesive team.

With her generous and courageous heart, she passionately described, "It's all about the team, Mom. He wants us to get together over the summer. He knows that we'll win if we work together and have great friendships. I think I'll organize a beach trip for everyone this summer."

The team concept brims with the hopefulness of belonging.

I love what research is saying about the team within our profession of education: collaboration is key. Relationships form the bedrock for the climb of learning.

Recently, we received a letter describing how our local university is transforming the practicum experience for student teachers. They were redesigning their program. They were modeling it after what the two student teachers experienced together within our learning community over the past year: collaboration. We were flattered.

The email provided the rationale:

> *Building capacity for collaboration and shared practice is vital for effective 21st Century teaching. Immersing teacher candidates in a collaborative professional context as part of their first teaching experience will provide a strong foundation for developing their teaching competency as a 'we' practice instead of an exclusively 'me' practice.*

The irony doesn't escape me; we are designing a collaborative practice for professionals to model belonging for children! We want teachers to have time to connect at the Table of Learning with each other, with parents, and with students.

We want rich classroom meetings, collaborative teaching teams, and shared responsibility for our learning community within our walls.

For us, a tremendously valuable connection within our halls and classrooms is the connection amongst our team of professional educators. We pray, sacrifice, advocate, champion, challenge, encourage, and support each other. Sometimes the label "collaboration" seems too simple. Our connections results in teachers who truly want to engage and create a unique and dynamic learning environment together.

We're authentic in our journey. It's human. It's real and raw.

With our honesty hats on, we also discuss how it is often difficult to celebrate each other's victories instead of feeling threatened or 'less than.' We discuss this awareness with the hopefulness of a heart held out in our hand.

Here is what we know for sure: great relationships are a recipe for student success! So we move towards each other. We break down classroom walls. We enjoy connecting like coffee on a spring morning.

When teachers are working together, they can do powerful things to improve their teaching and, in turn, improve student learning.

Learn Forward is not only inviting teachers to the Table of Learning to belong, but parents and students too!

The students will benefit from the active and warm relationships amongst the entire learning community.

Parents and teachers model the courage of teamwork to support a journey of belonging. In addition to modeling, we can also practice belonging in our homes and classrooms all over the world!

With just a few intentional choices, as a caregiver, I can help a child feel like they belong. I can:

- Catch their eyes and smile.

- Greet them warmly when they walk in the room.

- Give a hug.

- Cheer with authentic and 'just for you' praise.

- Reach out to the teacher/parent with a simple encouragement.

- Always hold high expectations and big grace.

- Keep working through challenges.

A child will learn how to create meaningful relationships and sustain them successfully over time. It will feel risky. It will feel hurtful. It is normal.

One practice of belonging we need to draw into our consciousness is the normal ebb and flow of relationships. Each friendship has a gentle moving towards and also a time to create more space or distance.

Again, the ebb and flow is normal, but tolerating it can be challenging. Complicated by the fact that children don't always have words for that process, so they can be dramatic or insensitive. The playground antics heat up.

I'm hopeful that parents and teachers can help children relate with one another better, understanding that relationships ebb and flow. It can happen with grace. We need words, modeling, and kindness.

Class meetings and family meetings are brilliant forums to practice the artfulness of relating with one another. There, we can ask powerful questions, listen to each other, role play, discuss, and continue to grow at the Table of Learning.

When all is said and done, happiness blooms in warm relationships.

The Grant Study of Harvard found over the last 75 years of studying 268 men that, "It is the capacity for intimate relationships that predicted flourishing in all aspects of these men's lives."

Learn Forward calls belonging the artfulness of creating meaningful relationships.

Learn Forward calls us all to courageously discover ways to create meaningful relationships! We can easily understand it as 'team.' When we connect with one another and empathize whole-heartedly, we can begin to find hopefulness and happiness in the world around us. It is a process and we call it: Learn Forward.

11

CHANGEMAKING

---

*Dear children, let us not love with words or speech
but with actions and in truth.*

I John 3:18

*That thing that keeps reminding you that there's more to life
than just going through life. That thing is your human spirit, the
extraordinary potential you were born with.*

*Your potential's waiting. Patiently.
Go. Use it. Make a conscious choice to be great.*

~ Luck Companies "Be Great" Video

Over the past few weeks, amidst my writing process, I was meditating on the paradox of "bold love." I'm curious about the duality.

"Bold love" is to be tender, empathetic, and soft-hearted, mixed with courage, capacity, and toughness. It is going out into the world to be your truest self, creating meaningful relationships and good along the way. To be successful in loving boldly, we must have a sense of worthiness in our pocket and hope for the greater good in our hands.

Changemaking is bold love.

> *Changemaking is a symphony of the five Learn Forward journeys, essential for all adults caring for children.*

This chapter shifts to a conscious consideration of how parents and teachers must become changemakers, embracing our fullest purpose on this planet, for the sake of the children.

In each of the journeys, we need to explore ourselves before we can illuminate them for our children and mindfully help them discover what matters most. So, as parents and teachers, we are destined to become changemakers.

Children will inevitably learn from our example and they will naturally embrace all of the journeys while in our care.

EXPLORE THE NEEDS AROUND YOU

While Learn Forward focuses on what is happening in North America, it is also informed by my worldwide inquiry into how to create the conditions for children to thrive.

I'm curious about the universal tenets. My personal exploration is shaped deeply by my work with the most vulnerable children of the world in East Africa through my charitable work.

Why do I travel each year to Africa? Leave my family? Sacrifice big chunks of my summer? Pay my way? Take Canadian volunteers? Risk?

Why do I eat foreign foods, deal with the side effects of malaria medication, fight with flesh-eating, insects and leave my pillow behind?

There are so many more 'why' questions.

I discover the answers by digging deeper into how I engage with the world, by noticing what I want to change and what motivates me to act. My personal changemaking journey illustrates how this works.

Do you ever wake up and not know where you are?

In this experience, there is a disorienting feeling, a frenetic spin of trying to ground, an urgency to settle the difference between dreaming and awakening. There is a panic to make sense of it. Then, you blink three times slowly, and the feeling goes away.

While I was in Uganda last summer, I had this experience. I woke up and needed to blink three times.

O yeah.

I realized.

I'm in Uganda.

I'm sleeping in a house dormitory at Kabojja International School. I am under a mosquito net on a foam mattress. I am looking out the window at the blooming bougainvillea bush.

Later that same day, I could easily orient because I sat at the Source Café in Jinja, Uganda, with an iced mocha, posting pictures on Facebook of teammates playing with the monkeys from our Nile boat trip. Sitting there felt enough like a tourist trip from my middle-class life that I could orient. I didn't need to blink. It was "normal," even in Africa.

But, when we drove deep into the tenements of Jinja to find a Niteo children's library for the poorest of children I was blinking again. I became disoriented when I saw their tattered clothes, infected eyes, and malnourished hair. I couldn't make sense of it.

It was just like waking up and not knowing where you are.

I can't begin to fathom how we live the way we do, and these dear sweet ones live in deprived, desperate, and diseased conditions.

The trick is (I'm going to say something extreme here), not to blink away extreme poverty! Don't blink it away!

Changemaking is about holding the difficult, the poor, the inhospitable, the diseased, and the damaged.

Why? Why do I do it?

I won't blink it away.

These children are trapped in a cycle of poverty and oppression. I know my own poverty. I won't turn my back on them!

As an educator, as a strategic thinker, as a mother, and as a human being, I must do what I can for these children, for the global good, for my own heart.

That's why.

Hold the discomfort. Hold the reality that children are living day in and day out in extreme poverty. If you do, your life will be changed forever.

We can each become changemakers in our own way. If we can tolerate the experience of the injustice, the inhospitable, and the inhumane for just a little while, we will be able to see how to take the next step forward and change the world.

When I hold my disorientation in those spaces, here's what happens:

I am motivated to make sustainable change.
I want to help the children of poverty in a
sustainable way. I believe in them. They aren't
a problem to be fixed; they are children to be
dignified. It is courageous. It is bold love!

I choose education as my platform. I could choose shoes, clothes, bicycles, or nutrition. I could bring medicine. But, what aligns most with who I am and offers the greatest chance of escape for these children is empowering them through education.

I partner with Ugandans. I stand with mothers, teachers, and caregivers to provide children with the gift of education. It isn't about my answers; it is about our relationship.

I invest in the future. A child reading unlocks imagination; imagination unlocks a new destiny. Education offers children living in poverty the greatest opportunity for escape. An education with essential literacies encourages a child to imagine, think critically, and create so they can live sustainably. So, I choose to send books, empower teachers, connect leaders, and create educational change.

It could be any need, hunger, or poverty. In the Learn Forward equation, changemaking is born out of holding the need we discover, unwaveringly. The gift of remembering the need encourages grit and determination. It invites creativity, optimism, and connection.

Don't blink it away.
Pause for a minute.
Make an offering.
It's an opportunity to effect change.
A call to change something that matters.

CHANGEMAKING, EVEN WHEN
THE STAR ISN'T SHINING

In Learn Forward, we use this made-up word to describe the journey when all things harmonize, and a child steps outside of themselves to serve the greater good: changemaking. I don't even want to hyphenate the word because it originates from the place of 'flow.'

I don't know about you, but sometimes I struggle with being in the 'flow' of life. Often, I'm wondering how to get through each day, moment-by-moment. There are demanding dynamics, created by big, bold expectations. I'm often trying to resist the temptation to fly into a full spin!

I want to be a changemaker, but I'm not sure how to fit it into my life.

A story from our home last Christmas offers the perfect picture.

We completed decorating the previous weekend. The stockings hung with care. But, you know the star, the star at the top of the tree; it didn't shine. My little one cried the next morning, "O no Mom! The star! It isn't shining!"

What do we do when the bulb is burnt out?

With all of our good intentions to be the light and change the world, our star isn't shining.

Have you ever held the beauty and the ashes, one in each hand? Have you ever felt on one hand, "I got this!" and on the other, "I've got no idea what I'm doing!" Have you lived in the tension?

I want to model changemaking.

I want my children to be changemakers.

And, the star doesn't work! Trapped by mundane details, we are distracted by the duties. We are not sure how to become who we want our children to become.

Here are three practices The Builder and I use to make space and refocus. It takes courage. We pause so we can embrace changemaking in our lives:

1. **We sit down.**

We have breakfast with the children. The Builder and I grab our coffee, delay the writing and working, and we connect. We take the time to nap, prioritize church, and explore our advent reading together. We talk lots. He calls it "getting on the same page." I like it.

2. **We let it go.**

The house still isn't clean from the tornado of life. The children still aren't perfectly coiffed. We aren't getting everything done or attending all of the events we planned for this week. We just smile, and The Builder says to me, "We're doin' good." Our hearts feel the sense of freedom that will release us into what matters most.

3. **We model what we hope.**

We continually ask ourselves, "How can we express love to those around us?" We reach out. We get involved in our community locally, and we pursue relationships, even imperfectly. We invest in our teams, and we invest in our charities of choice. We consider the simple gifts. We give them. We receive too! We are grateful.

Over time, we see clear illustrations of the change in our hearts and the hearts of our children. We point out the little miracles. We celebrate them privately around our Table.

Our hearts change as we go about our days.

> *Changemakers are born in the ordinary; that's what makes it extraordinary.*

If you're hoping to see your children as changemakers, take heart!

We can set the intention and experience it in the ordinariness, despite the fact that sometimes the star doesn't shine!

CHANGEMAKERS ARE VIBRANT HUMAN BEINGS

When I started Niteo Africa, I was not a vibrant human being. I was amidst a treacherous and devastating time in my life. Creating was wildly dysfunctional. While people warned me that I should let the Niteo dream die, I didn't, I couldn't.

What I could do was get healthy. I took a year off work. I dove into therapy, took up yoga, took beach chairs to the sand and read books. I was learning about my relationships and deeply reflective. I listened to what was working and what wasn't working. I traversed the ugly mountain of shame and found great courage in being a mother.

While Niteo's birth was painful and challenging, we recovered together and became healthier.

From these broken shards of life, I share with conviction about becoming a changemaker and modeling the journey for all children.

Here's what helped me take courage to reach out and choose thriving and changemaking.

SELF-CARE

I learned self-care the hard way. When I think about lifelong changemakers I admire, it is the teacher, caregiver, or parent who knows the golden rule of "love your neighbor as yourself" and lives with a commitment to thriving.

Self-care is an essential ingredient for vibrant service.

Kristen Neff's work on self-compassion informs my idea of cultivating and practicing gentleness with self. We are all in a process. When we accept imperfection, we more readily embrace risk-taking and changemaking.

Professionals and parents who exercise, eat well, bring joy to their days, and pursue healthy habits bring lifeblood to their work. Those who take the time to bring meaning and creativity to their lives through relationships, hobbies, and pursuits offer more to the children around them.

Oh! And, let's remember our sense of humor! It helps more than we realize.

If you can pace yourself with compassion and self-care, you can sustain the vibrant energy you need to take the risks necessary to change the world!

BE DOGGEDLY DEDICATED

Teachers, parents, and humanitarians who see their work as a calling are vibrant. They inspire changemaking all around them, particularly in the lives of the children they nurture.

Once I interviewed a teacher, and she passionately declared to me, "I was made to be a Kindergarten teacher!" I knew right then I would hire her. She served Kindergarten students for twenty years. We can follow her dedication!

Being dedicated must only be tempered by self-care.

And, don't get me wrong there are still "dog days." Days when being vibrant looks like asking for help, sharing challenges, asking for advice, caring, praying, or brainstorming unseen solutions.

The key is to sustain; be doggedly dedicated.

BE A LIFELONG LEARNER

Learn Forward is most fully realized in the changemaking journey because we must be continuous learners to sustain changemaking. The most vibrant models for children are always reflecting on practice, inquiring, setting ambitious goals, reading, learning, and initiating growth.

They aren't afraid to try new things because they realize everyone is a learner!

Lifelong learning is action oriented and in some ways insatiable. It intelligently asks questions and continues to iterate on solutions.

Vibrant professionals and parents embrace change and acknowledge the rapidly evolving pedagogy of life around us!

BE ORGANIZED AND EFFICIENT

Teachers are some of the most organized, efficient, and orderly people I know, even the very creative and spontaneous types!

They know how to manage space for form and function. They know how to foster a learning environment that honors community and includes expectations for being together. They develop routines and systems that contribute to children's independence, creativity, and collaboration. It is a beautiful thing to behold, and I learn so much from them!

I think as parents, we can learn from this example. I am not a naturally organized person. I am a big-picture thinker, lack discipline, and enjoy being creative. However, over time, I am learning forward. Through reading books, following excellent examples, and the support of my dear husband, I am becoming more organized and efficient. It's what encourages my growth as a changemaker alongside the children!

What we choose to do daily has the greatest potential to change the world.

What changes can you harness into your days that will make the world a better place?

WORKING IN TEAMS

We can't survive and thrive without each other. We must connect and create a network of like-minded and inspiring friendships or teams around us.

As teachers, we can survive in the classroom by ourselves, but we can thrive in a community where different gifts and abilities add spice and challenge our thinking.

It is the same for parents.

Let's discuss this further in the next section on the Table of Learning.

CULTIVATING MEANING

At the end of the day, to become a changemaker, we must understand that it is all a faith journey filled with the messiness of humanity. It is a journey of self-reflection and intellectual honesty. We must make meaning of the needs around us.

It is a faith journey of capturing the moments of victory, reminding oneself "I am enough," and having the grace to remember, "Tomorrow is a fresh start."

VIBRANT TEAMS CREATE CHANGE

When I think about how each of us becomes changemakers, I am profoundly moved by memories of all my vibrant teams. I think of my public school team in Orange, California. I think of my Niteo Africa team of humanitarians. I think of The Builder's teams creating whole communities. I think of my Willowstone Academy team of dedicated and talented professionals.

Becoming energetic and alive individually helps us create and participate in vibrant teams. We move past exhaustion. We take responsibility for our energy. We model changemaking, and our children follow suit.

Vibrant teams lead change.

Participating with and contributing to a dynamic team is a great act of belonging and changemaking.

The world shifts on its axis because of our micro-movements.

My world is filled with teams right now! Everywhere I look, I can see teamwork spilling out onto the pages of my life. I can see it in families, classrooms, professional relationships, humanitarian work, athletics, and academics.

My big kids and their cousins are all competing and performing at the high levels that high school and university afford. For the first time last weekend, the little one's dance class performed in an ensemble.

My students are competing and performing in everything from Battle of the Books to the spring "Leo the Lion" creative arts performance. I'm working on preparing for Niteo Team 2015's humanitarian trip to Uganda.

The Builder and I work with talented professional teams navigating the rapid pace of change in our 21st Century culture.

The following principles of Team encourage changemaking:

FAMILY IS A CHILD'S FIRST TEAM.

Children identify with their first team, their family. The hearts in our family are knit together because we do life in concert. As a mom, I know no one can love my children as much as I do. We are a team. So, we use teamwork language for our "Family Team." We talk about cheering, working together, and team norms. We schedule team meetings to talk about the "practices and big games" of life. We are creating a team in our homes.

EVEN OUR BROKEN FAMILIES CAN BRING LIFE!

Recently, I had the wonderful opportunity to get to know some new friends. As we related, a successful and gorgeous woman told me about her difficult experiences as a child in a fatherless existence. She talked about how her older sister had courageously held the hands-on parenting role while her mom worked three jobs. At the end of her story, I struggled to connect how a woman from such a broken background could lead such a changemaking life. She told me, "Hope. Karine, all we need is hope."

Cultivating hope is always the greatest contribution we can make to our team.

TOGETHER, PARENTS AND EDUCATORS CAN CREATE TRANSFORMATION

No one can do it alone. It takes a village.

My soul experiences a drink of great love when parents and educators come together to share hearts for the sake of the children.

I know it takes time. No one has much time. But, that's why Learn Forward is so revolutionary because we focus on what matters most. This week, in my office, as Chief Learning Officer of Willowstone Academy, I sat with a family with some big questions. We held a space of hopefulness.

It was the Table of Learning and it was life giving.

I know I will have this opportunity several more times before the end of the year, as we work towards all that remains. Let's reach towards developing a team with a fierce tenderness.

TEAMWORK IS HOW WE CULTIVATE BELONGING AND CHANGEMAKING.

We can only change the world together! We can only be together if we choose togetherness! We can choose togetherness by bravely accepting each other as we are.

What I know for sure:

1. Teamwork is choosing to belong with others.

2. Choosing our teams wisely is how we intentionally shape our lives.

3. Children are practicing teamwork in many ways.

4. Teamwork is the most powerful force for creativity and changemaking in the world.

We can change the world with a team.

Together, let's heed Victoria Safford's encouragement,

> Our mission is to plant ourselves at the gates of hope~
> ...the piece of ground from which you see the world both as it is and
> as it could be, as it might be, as it will be; the place from which
> you glimpse not only struggle, but joy in the struggle and we stand
> there, beckoning and calling, telling people what we are seeing,
> asking people what they see.

Vibrant, hopeful teams create change.

Let's cultivate belonging with the intention of serving the greater good on an active changemaking journey. It is a courageous, Learn Forward journey.

CHANGEMAKING ARISES FROM OUR DEEPEST HUNGERS

When I met Miranda in early 2013, we were standing in our delightfully decorated Kindergarten classroom at Willowstone Academy. During her tour, she told me about her boys. She spoke eloquently about their strengths and shared just a sliver of her hopes for what a school could provide. She was obviously a thoughtful and devoted mother.

I could feel her fatigue from the system; we all feel trapped at times.

Everyone can resonate. Our culture, our schools, our communities, our relationships aren't always thriving.

She was standing in the gap between what is and what could be. She wanted something more for her boys. Neither of us had words for it.

After she enrolled her boys at Willowstone Academy, she approached me in the fall and began to share. Our hopes for education began to spill out at the Table with the aroma of motherhood and our professional perspectives mixing.

We started where we were: our school.

Miranda brought her thoughtful and elegant insight as an entrepreneur, coach, and communicator. I brought my experience as a passionate educator driving to create something unique.

Over time, we dove into describing the depth of our learning community. We wanted to create a meaningful expression of who Willowstone Academy is as a learning community: our lived experience and abiding beliefs. We wanted change.

The teachers, students, and parents gathered around the Table and followed Miranda's lead into the process of penning our Willowstone Academy Manifesto. Every member of our community was invited. It wasn't a fundraiser or a band concert; it was the richest and most meaningful experience within a learning community I've experienced to date.

Our Manifesto continues to be a pillar of our learning community, offering the strength of imagery and language to provide structure and form: rooted in faith, hope, and love.

The children went on to write classroom manifestos with their teachers.

It was a bold and grand innovation in cultivating a culture bathed in our belief: the extraordinary potential of every child.

Our school's online platform and videos were next, but it wasn't completely satiating our desire to get to the heart of what really matters for children.

We kept meeting. Miranda would bring powerful questions. I would speak from my heart. It was a season of writing and creating. We were both motivated by the heart of changemaking.

Changemaking lives in every heart and needs to find its expression. Changemaking arises from our deepest hunger.

Learn Forward is changemaking.

The summer before the printing of this book, I found a holy ground and Learn Forward took shape. I sketched the five most important journeys into my journal. The journeys are championing the children.

Universally, Learn Forward is dedicated to seeing children thriving.

Our desire is to help:

1. School faculties create environments and cultures where children encounter goodness and can take a more natural path towards greatness.

2. Parents create a home life for children where connections thrive. We want children to grow up in homes where parents feel encouraged and emboldened in their sacred work.

3. Educators, parents, and students to feel courageous on their journey! Then, we can develop learning communities where we can ask questions, share experiences and stand together, holding the mysteries and the possibilities.

Learn Forward believes in changemaking.

I am grateful for the journey of belonging and changemaking that Miranda and I took together.

It led us to Learn Forward.

CHILDREN AND CHANGEMAKING

I see it all around me! Children are taking up the mantle of changing our world: caring about their brother and sister, the planet, and the far-off friend. They are inspired and determined.

Today my big girl booked her flight to spend a month of her 17-year old summer serving children in orphanages in Haiti. She is brimming over with generosity.

I realize my one child is not a sample size large enough for the Learn Forward model, but she is not alone. The youth are concerned, inspired, and taking action.

This week the newly formed, student-organized Eco Team met with me at my school. They want to compost and grow a garden of organic vegetables for their school canteen. They are willing to fundraise to get it.

Children as changemakers are unafraid.

Their faith is abundant! They believe they can make a difference. They want their lives to be about a grander purpose.

As teachers and parents, we can guide them, offer them support, and ensure we are modeling the way.

Children are changemakers.

When we link arms with enthusiasm and vibrant hopefulness, we can change the world! There may be difficult days when the 'star' isn't shining, but we can hold onto each other and our faith in the restoration of all things. Then, we will have the courage to act with goodness towards humanity. Learn Forward is about a deep commitment to make this world a better place.

PART FOUR
the table of learning

12

A LEARNING COMMUNITY IS LIKE BEING AT A TABLE

*Coming together is a beginning; keeping together
is progress; working together is success.*

~ Henry Ford

Words are powerful. We need new words and imagery in our
collective imagination to suggest new ways of being in our homes,
schools, and communities. We need words and metaphors to
transform our current learning communities; metaphors to
provide vision of reaching out, taking risks, and innovating
together. We must envision a new kind of relationship with each
other in our schools and for our children.

On the sea of change, we can only sail with certainty if we are
together. Education needs to prepare children for an ever-
changing future that we cannot see.

It is paramount to focus on competencies, process, and relationships within our schools.

We must develop a new relationship with technology with a vision to serve our children, homes, and classrooms. The future requires a new vision for being together and building community.

With the five most important journeys of a child present in my consciousness,

I describe the profoundly courageous and truly tender relationship between child, parent, and educator as the Table of Learning.

My father gave me *The Courage to Teach* by Parker Palmer a decade ago. When I read it, I resonated deeply with Parker Palmer's notion of the "third thing, a great thing, at the center of the pedagogical circle."

If I pause to consider the metaphor, I would love to think of the Table of Learning as fit for a king, with learning at the center, dignified and elegant. We would all pursue learning with valor and nobility.

Honestly though, the relationships between teachers, students, and parents look more like our kitchen tables in a typical North American home.

The Table of Learning is set with 'real life' and evidence of hard work. It is fortified with the commitment of connections and at ease with the messiness of humanity.

The metaphor of a kitchen dinner table connotes a certain intimacy, authenticity, and dedication. Sharing at the dinner table sets the tone for the relationships in schools. The child, the parent, and the educator sit around the Table, each as learners, each as courageous participants, each being nourished.

The barriers come down between us as we learn to listen with open hearts and faith. Each of us has something to offer.

Partnering hand-in-hand at the Table of Learning results in the personalization of learning and facilitates the changes necessary in education!

Is it an ideal? Of course it is. But, we must hold ideals with boldness.

The bounty will be realized in schools, in homes, and in our children when we navigate change from the Table of Learning.

Here are five ways school relationships are like being at a Table of Learning:

1. **Learning is at the centre.**

I often think of our learning community as a great thing, a Table, with learning at the center. No one individual is at the center of the Table; the learning is. We are all learners in the 21st Century notion. No one is the single-handed expert. We all need to approach the Table as learners. That is a profound shift.

The learning must be visible to all at the Table.

During the years I worked with FreshGrade, an Edtech software development company interested in documenting and communicating learning in schools, we were asking how to make a child's learning visible. It was powerful. We were interested in how to improve the experience of assessment and reporting for teachers, parents, and students.

What emerged was a digital portfolio tool for documenting learning between students, teachers, and parents. Report cards and one meeting per year can't achieve our dream for the Table of Learning, but we have powerful technologies at our disposal to help us now. I have hope for the future.

Of course, it isn't just a child who is learning at the Table. Each of us has a responsibility to learn and grow with reciprocity.

2.   **Parents play an essential role at the table.**

Of course, we all know, when parents participate in their child's education students thrive. I can easily see this trend in our daily practice at Willowstone Academy. If parents and educators sit at the Table together with students, progress accelerates immeasurably. We value the learning and the process. We collaborate. We communicate effectively. Children progress towards their extraordinary potential.

As an educator, I realize parental involvement takes time and energy from teachers and parents. Time and energy aren't in abundance in our culture. So, we have to make a concerted effort to carve out time. Because the parent's role is essential, at Willowstone Academy, we are setting the intention to orient ourselves at the Table. We are ensuring teachers have time to connect thoughtfully with parents over personalized learning goals, portfolio celebrations, and through the daily use of FreshGrade.

We want to create space for meaningful conversations on each child's growth and development with the student and the parent. We want to make meaning of the learning together. We want to empower the student to own their personal learning journey.

3. Sometimes it looks like a "real" table.

It can get messy. It isn't perfect. Things spill or sometimes there's too much salt. Someone doesn't show up or it is awkward. I love this metaphor during the authentic human experiences when our relationships don't look perfect. In those moments I like to ask,

"What is the most essential learning for this Table right now?"

Dare-I-say, it might not be the curriculum goals.

4. Every meal is different.

I don't know about your family, but despite our commitment to sit down twice per day together, it looks different from day-to-day. Even today I chose to be late to an appointment because my teenage son made it up to breakfast (albeit late). I stayed a few more moments to connect with him.

It happens at school too. Sometimes we can't include the parents at the Table for one reason or another. The learning goals shift or we need to add a specialist or a new assessment to inform us. At the Table, there are different visitors, family members, and menu changes each day. We are accustomed to change. It bolsters our courage to be together.

5. Celebrate hospitality!

With a faith in the re-creation of all things, we can be hospitable towards each other. When our hearts are steadfast in our sense of self and belonging, we can join the Table of Learning with openness and curiosity. It's a new idea. It is full of the ancient notion of hospitality and welcoming.

Parker Palmer also teaches,

> *Hospitality rightly understood is premised on the notion that the stranger has much to teach us. It actively invites 'otherness' into our lives to make them more expansive, including forms of otherness that seem utterly alien to us. Of course, we will not practice deep hospitality if we do not embrace the creative possibilities inherent in our differences.*

It requires something from everyone. Everyone must be responsible for focusing on what matters most.

And while every meal at the Table doesn't look perfect, the value and the process of being together are worthy of celebration! We don't get it right every time, but we continue to gather and build relationships, holding our learning with reverence.

Teachers, parents, and students, let's join the feast!

13

THE POSTURE OF A LEARNER

The Table of Learning is for the student, parent, and educator. It is a nourishing affair.

At the Table, our hearts are in a posture of humility. My yogi friend calls it a beginner's mind.

In a sense, we are all coming to the Table open to new possibilities like children, full of faith, hope, and love. At the Table, we are nourished and inspired for more of life!

We must be intentional about preparing our hearts to be at the Table of Learning together and embracing a beginner's mind.

For example, as each new school year dawns, summer whispers it won't stay forever, and I begin the gradual journey back into a more formal routine. I relish a reflective journey back to school, much more than the standard school supply shopping or the "9 Ways to Get Your Child Ready for School." The truth is I need to prepare my heart to be at the Table of Learning!

It happens year round. It is focusing on,

How can I take the posture of a learner?

Preparation is much less about what I 'do' and much more about 'being.'

Here are some attitudes or postures to help educators, parents and students navigate school days together. Hopefully, they provide you with some key reflections you can use in September and throughout the school year!

Cultivate enthusiasm about learning.

Our children will drink in our attitudes about learning and school. If we share our excitement about the process, they will mirror our delight, especially as young children. Even parents of teenagers should not underestimate their influence!

There's lots of time at the Table.

While it never feels like there's enough time from day-to-day or month-to-month, there is lots of time for the growth and development of children. Rome wasn't built in a day and children aren't done learning at the end of a school year. June is just an arbitrary resting point. Learning is a life-long journey.

Whatever is left undone at the end of a school year creates an opportunity for the future. Fear rushes, but we can posture our hearts knowing that nothing is wasted. We can be at ease with our focus on what matters most.

ACTIVELY DISCOVER HOW YOUR CHILD OR STUDENT LEARNS BEST.

Curiosity about your child's learning journey will be such a gift of support to your child. Two things will happen.

First, you'll have an opportunity to authentically encourage your child, from the trenches of learning. I know I love it when people say to me, "I know this is hard, let's figure it out together!"

Second, when you engage in what they are learning, you will gain insights in the process. The insights you glean will be an asset you can bring to the Table to collaborate.

BE WILLING TO CONSIDER DIFFERENT PERSPECTIVES.

Everyone deserves a voice at the Table of Learning. No one should be silenced or unheard.

In school communities, we need to open the gates and dine together. We will share and listen. We will embrace each worthy perspective at the Table of Learning.

Allow me to explain.

Educators and parents each offer valuable insights into children based on experience.

Educators are experienced and typically know a particular age range well. Also, they observe the children in a demanding learning and social environment each day. They are able to provide an objective perspective that is otherwise very difficult for a parent to perceive.

Likewise, parents are the experts on their child. Moms, Dads, and Guardians are holding the primary responsibility and have a deep inner wisdom to offer. We need to genuinely welcome parents into the process. I realize there are profound barriers including language, time, schedules, capacity, among others; it is courageous to continue to press forward for our ideal.

The challenge is to listen deeply to each other, over time, for the sake of the children.

When I sit at the Table of Learning as a mother, sometimes it feels like standing under Niagara Falls. I have so much emotion and affection for my child; I become a little less objective. I remain at the Table, with an open heart, as my child's advocate and expert.

When I sit at the Table of Learning as an educator, I have a lifelong commitment to the best interests of children, so I deeply desire effective communication for the sake of the student. Both are passionate positions.

Teachers have so much to offer parents. Parents have so much to offer teachers. We must learn to listen to each other.

Dare we get trapped in our communication; deceived into believing the adults can figure it out.

Most importantly, we must hear the child. What is the child communicating with words and behaviour? We must truly assess and integrate what the child is showing us and telling us. We must believe in the child's innate capacity for learning and growth. We must honour their journey, perspectives, and thoughts.

At every age, the conversation about learning is enhanced when the student owns the learning journey and shares it confidently at the Table of Learning.

I deeply value the insights gleaned at the Table of Learning for each one of my children, and I have one graduating, one in preschool, and one in between. Each opportunity to connect at the Table of Learning is a gift to our family, and I welcome the opportunity to dine together. I know I'm going to learn for sure! Most of all, I want to listen to my children and nourish their journeys.

Thoughtful conversations and a kind-hearted approach are hallmarks of being at the Table of Learning.

We will abide with one another, we will learn, and we will shimmer in our expansiveness!

14

ABIDING AT THE TABLE OF LEARNING

If we are coming to the Table of Learning, we must learn to abide.

I revisit the commitment to abide at the Table every fall. Fall is the season of plenty. It is the season of gratitude. The school year is full of the optimism of beginnings.

However, my world doesn't always fit neatly into the hopefulness and idealism I love to swirl around in my mind for inspiration and intoxication. What happens when the Table of Learning isn't working? What happens when trust looks like the peeling paint on an old dappled barn?

In our learning community, here is what we do to work together courageously for the sake of the children when everything doesn't neatly fit into our designed packages.

1. Keep Children Safe

We focus on the fundamental needs of children. We discuss sleeping and nutrition; we work to keep hearts soft and bodies safe. We don't underestimate the power of the basics. And, I have science to back up my mother's common sense.

2. Take Time to Be Together

When things are bumping along or even tumbling down into a crevasse, we must make the time to be together.

My best weeks include the blessing of coming to the Table of Learning with parents individually, in small groups, and in large events.

Some connections offer the opportunity for private, heartfelt meetings to address unique needs, restore relationships, or learn more about each other.

Most notably at Willowstone Academy, we host meetings with parents to explore values and vision in broad brushstrokes. We include students and parents in meaningful conversations about the culture of our learning community. When members of our community have an opportunity to dialogue in respectful and whole-hearted ways about what matters most, we create health.

3. Reaffirm our Values Together

It's not always easy to hold onto values in a shifting and organic learning community. It requires standing in the gap, in a struggle between the ideal of perfection and the challenging realities.

As an example, we value meeting the needs of children in a personalized way with strong attachments and big doses of attention. Student-educator ratios are important in this value.

However, it isn't always perfectly in proportion, so we have to struggle in the gap between the ideal and the real. Because of the gap, we must abide at the Table of Learning and state our values. Where are we commonly committed?

4. Cultivate a Culture of Continuous Growth

When things can't be perfect, we ask, "How can they be better?" While it isn't always flawless, as a community, we can always make an effort to be better.

5. Keep Asking Questions

Learn Forward is deeply committed to asking powerful questions. It is in our DNA. Part of abiding at the Table of Learning, means we continue to ask powerful questions.

How can we improve? How can we empower the student? What is propelling our learning forward? What do I need to learn? What do I need to hear? Where do I need to soften my heart? Where do I need the courage to accept or forgive?

Sometimes the most important step we can take is asking a powerful question prompting positive change.

6. Brainstorm

We explore new possibilities, connections, and opportunities. Brainstorming requires us to approach the Table with an open mind and heart so new ideas can emerge.

I love it when a team member sends me a Saturday email of brainstorms or we solve problems collaboratively in the hallway. I particularly appreciate when our hearts come together to hold what is yet unsolved.

7. Encourage Each Other's Hearts

Within our community, we are mindful of what others are going through in their lives, homes, and classrooms. We cry with, pray for, and lean on each other. We are a community of learners.

15

A RISING TIDE RAISES ALL SHIPS

Education is in a sea of change. Parents and educators know it.

Often, I have the privilege of sitting with bright and dedicated minds to discuss education. A more rare privilege includes sitting with someone who deeply understands the educational systems in the West, along with those in East Africa with breadth. I am grateful for these rare opportunities because they offer me a glimpse of what is universal for children and society.

Bright minds understand we are amidst a sea of transformation. It is universal. It will require courage. There is no debate. The question is the same, "What principles of change are universal?"

I share the following themes to suggest universal principles of change for the transformation of education. These themes are pillars of the Learn Forward Table.

3 CS—CULTURES OF CONTINUOUS CHANGE

The words 'continuous improvement' are used around the world and what resonates with me is the word 'transformation!' The enemy of transformation is conformity.

Within education, we need to adopt the willingness to think outside-the-box, to risk, to challenge, to fail, to iterate.

We must do this together from the foundation of the Table of Learning.

The rate of this change will happen faster if everyone understands we must think and work differently, learn and grow. The local learning community must move forward together to create this type of environment.

EVERYONE IS AT THE TABLE OF LEARNING

We must all become learners to adopt a change mindset for transformation: students, parents, teachers, and community members. I don't just mean casually dipping our toes into this idea of growth every-once-in-awhile. We all must pursue progress.

Learning keeps us creative, encourages risk-taking, and creates a collaborative learning community.

It includes everything from working on action-research within our practice to dedicating ourselves to listening and learning from our students each day.

If we can keep learning central on our Table, our communities will navigate the sea of change.

LEADERSHIP WILLING TO RISK

While the heart of change is in the classroom, leaders must risk pushing forward into unknown territory.

While much is being written on how to prepare students for the future, there are still many questions about how to do that effectively or what a 21st Century classroom should look like.

Educational leadership must support the emergence and risks of the teacher; likewise, parents must support the emergence and risks of the school and classroom.

We all must allow for individual personalities to take initiative and be innovative. Leadership throughout the community will unlock the potential of transformation.

EDUCATORS AT THE HEART

While there may be a vigorous debate about this, I believe that teachers are at the heart of all educational change.

While leaders play an important role, and the students' self-directed pursuit of learning should be the outcome, the shift must happen in the hearts and minds of the classroom teacher.

For teachers, the first 'bite of the elephant' is the belief that things can change! We need supportive parents with open hearts at the Table to make it safe enough to try.

SUPPORTIVE COLLABORATION

Within a context of rapid change, nothing is more important than an emotionally nurturing and supportive environment to establish a sustainable culture of change.

Remember our Belonging chapter?

In our school community, support ranges from quick hallway chats to Mindfulness Mondays, from devotions to professional learning communities.

I am grateful for the supportive team I have both in my brick-and-mortar school and my professional learning network. Without a sense of community, the pressures could easily overwhelm. I hold great gratitude for the team at Willowstone Academy.

When we all open our hands, we realize:

A rising tide raises all ships,
particularly on the sea of change.
Take courage!

PART FIVE
learn forward in practice

16

THE FIVE JOURNEYS AT HOME

Where do you begin to explore the five journeys at home, with your partner and children?

The questions on the following pages are meant to help you begin exploring the five journeys at home. This is where you shape what matters most to your family with greater clarity.

I encourage you to listen to what your heart and your child's heart whispers with an open mind. I hope your exploration here leads to deepening your connections and cultivating more joy.

Some of the questions may feel daunting, abstract or stir up uncertainty. My invitation to you is to lean into what matters most and go with the ideas that come first. There are no right or wrong answers. You can always circle back and change.

FAITH

Your thoughts are inspired. Write whatever comes to mind. Be as specific as possible.

1.   What does faith mean to a child? How do they capture it? What is essential to your child?

2.   Considering a season of difficulty or surrender in the past, how did you "fall into faith?"

3.   What supported you? What was your prayer? What was your best self-talk?

4.   What is your deep hunger? What is your child's deep hunger? How are they satiated?

5.   How did you practice faith in your family of origin? How do you currently practice faith? How do your children respond to your practice of faith?

6.   In teaching children to achieve, we must teach them to believe! We can teach them through powerful metaphors, poetry, stories of faith, nature, and modeling. Consider particular literature, routines, mantras, inspirational materials, experiences in nature, rituals, or spiritual practices that are working in your home. Write them down.

7. What do you want your children to believe as they enter adulthood? What is transformative about those beliefs? How will you intentionally show you value those beliefs in your own life? How will you practice your beliefs this year?

8. How does faith support us in creating meaningful relationships or belonging? Where do you experience powerful community as a family? What are you investing in that community?

9. Name the powerful concepts, such as forgiveness and acceptance, that flow from your faith.

10. It takes faith to dream. What is your dream for your life? What is your dream for your family?

11. As you consider faith, describe any shifts you experience in your inner world.

Now reread your responses and highlight or underline any responses, words or phrases that deeply resonate.

WORTHINESS

Your thoughts are inspired. Write whatever comes to mind. Be as specific as possible.

1. Describe when you feel a sense of dignity and worth. When does your child?

2. What words does your heart need to hear? How can you share those messages with your child? Who else is speaking those messages to your child?

3. My faith helps me understand the profound concepts of forgiveness and acceptance. Because of this understanding, I know my faith expands my sense of worthiness. What expands your sense of worthiness? What inspires you?

4. What is unfinished in your child? How can you extend a gentle compassion towards what is unfinished? Write a one-sentence message of comfort to them. How can you creatively communicate that message to them? What helps you remember that there is more time to learn?

5. Name a major achievement in your life. How did you make it? How did you overcome the obstacles? How did you continue forward under the pressure? How did you climb that mountain of pursuit?! How can you share this story with your child this week?

6. Describe your courageous ideal in handling failure in your home. Write down three practical ways you can infuse your home with the notion that "failure" is a stone on a path to mastery?

7.   When we elevate process over a product, we offer children the opportunity to learn grit, tenacity, and perseverance. How can you 'cheer for the swing' in authentic ways in your home?

8.   What character traits or nobility are worthy in your child's heart? How can you see those character traits manifesting in your child's life? How does your awareness of their uniqueness enhance your relationship?

Now reread your responses and highlight or underline any responses, words or phrases that deeply resonate.

SELFHOOD

Your thoughts are inspired. Write whatever comes to mind. Be as specific as possible.

1. What does your child need to learn in the next year that is beyond the curriculum? What is your role in teaching? How can you creatively partner with your child's teacher to achieve these goals?

2. What are your child's unique and special qualities?

3. What are your child's interests or passions?

4. When was the last time your child showed a growing sense of independence, agency, initiative, or creativity? How did you support their journey with safety?

5. What practices in your home demonstrate you are 'crazy' about your child? What practices could you implement?

6. What do you need to thrive? List everything. Be specific. Why would modeling thriving be powerful? What would you need to change to become a better model?

7. If you are in survival mode, how can you take concrete steps this week, this month, and this year to move to a more grounded and stable place?

8.   What are the signs your child is NOT thriving? Why aren't they thriving? Hint: It isn't always what they tell you. For example, your child could be saying they are struggling because kids are mean on the playground, but the truest reason is that they didn't get enough sleep or eat properly that day.

9.   What is your child day-dreaming about? Imagining? What are the areas of growth your child's teacher is naming? How can you support growing independence in those areas?

10. In a family meeting, ask your child what support he or she might need from you to complete homework independently. Build a routine you all agree upon in advance.

11. What systems do you need in place in your home to ensure you are holding your child accountable for independence, effort, and completion?

12. When do you feel most courageous? When does your child feel most courageous?

Now reread your responses and highlight or underline any responses, words or phrases that deeply resonate.

BELONGING

Your thoughts are inspired. Write whatever comes to mind. Be as specific as possible.

1. Belonging represents the journey of creating meaningful relationships. What are your most treasured relationships? Why?

2. How does your child demonstrate empathy?

3. How do you practice investing in a community? Why? What do you have to give up or surrender? What do you gain?

4. Where does your child feel confident and at ease in relationships? Where does your child experience belonging?

5. How can you nurture acceptance and forgiveness in your child's heart as they navigate friendship? How can you support your child to cultivate a sense of personal boundaries and sense of self in friendships?

6. Parker Palmer writes about how hospitality is being with and welcoming someone different from oneself. How can you infuse your child's experience of the world with a sense of hospitality?

7. Tell a story of your child's courage in friendship.

8. How can you court your child into the safety of your arms, as you inspire them to reach out towards communities and others with a bright boldness?

9. Belonging can happen in schools. When does your child feel like he or she belongs at school?

10. Describe your schedule for family meetings. What is on your agenda for the next meeting?

Now reread your responses and highlight or underline any responses, words or phrases that deeply resonate.

CHANGEMAKING

Your thoughts are inspired. Write whatever comes to mind. Be as specific as possible.

1. "Make a conscious choice to be great." What is greatness? What is greatness in your family?

2. It takes courage to consider changemaking. Where do you feel afraid? How can you move forward with the courage of a child?

3. What micro-changes do you need to make in your home? As parents? As children? Are they empowering?

4. Who embodies "bold love" as a changemaker in your family, community, or network?

5. What does it mean to you to 'hold the need you discover, unwaveringly?' Write a list of needs you have discovered in your learning community. Circle one or two you feel passionate about holding. How can you hold those needs as important over the next month? Over the next year?

6. How do you serve the 'greater good' even when your star doesn't shine? How do you move towards health and wholeness in a way that honors yourself and others?

7.   What is the role of self-care and self-compassion in your life as you serve others?

8.   Name the three most re-creating self-care strategies that release you further into changemaking.

9.   What is sustainable change? What inspires you to take action to invest in sustainable change?

10. If vibrant teams lead change, how can you invest in the team around you? How can your family take on one or two rituals of a team that will empower change?

11. Your learning community needs you! How can you support the creation of rich and meaningful experiences within your community?

12. What great and powerful ideas come to life in your child's eyes as you discuss the idea of becoming a changemaker with him or her?

Now reread your responses and highlight or underline any responses, words or phrases that deeply resonate. Create one Learn Forward practice that you can implement this week to help you focus on what matters most.

What happened? We would love to hear your story. Just use *#LFstories* to share on your social media channels or blog.

WANT TO DIVE DEEPER INTO DESIGNING A HOME LIFE WHERE CONNECTIONS THRIVE?

If you and your partner would like more information about working with a Learn Forward coach send a note to hello@learnforward.ca. To learn more about Nest-Building courses and retreats, visit: www.learnforward.ca.

17

THE FIVE JOURNEYS AT SCHOOL

Where do you begin to explore the five journeys at school, with your colleagues and students?

The questions on the following pages are meant to help you begin exploring the five journeys at school. This is where you shape what matters most for your students with greater clarity.

I encourage you to listen to the whispers of your heart and students with an open mind. I hope your exploration here leads to deepening your connections and cultivating more joy in your practice.

Some of the questions may feel daunting, abstract or stir up uncertainty. My invitation to you is to lean into what matters most and go with the ideas that come first. There are no right or wrong answers. You can always circle back and change.

FAITH

Your thoughts are inspired. Write whatever comes to mind. Be as specific as possible.

1. What does faith mean for a child? How do they capture it? Could it be essential?

2. Do you agree with the Learn Forward definition of faith as...
    ...an experience of comfort.
    ...a deep belief in the restoration of all things.
    ...a whispered invitation of hopefulness.
    ...a beckoning to the dance of life!
    Why or why not? What would you change? How does your definition inform your teaching practice?

3. What challenges or difficulties are your students experiencing? What beliefs will carry them through those challenges? How can you infuse your classroom with those beliefs?

4. What are your deepest hungers? What are your students'
    deepest hungers? How are they satiated?

5. Think broadly, how do you currently practice faith? It could
    be experiences in nature, practices of honouring your own
    self-worth, investments into community, prayers, creative
    work, or formal religious rituals. Why are your practices
    important to your sacred work as an educator?

6. In teaching children to achieve, we must teach them to
    believe! You can teach them through powerful metaphors,
    poetry, stories of faith, nature, and modeling. Consider
    particular literature, routines, mantras, inspirational
    materials, experiences in nature, rituals, or spiritual
    practices that are working in your classroom. Write them
    down.

7.   What do you want your students to believe when they are grown? What is transformative about those beliefs? How will you intentionally show you value those beliefs in your own life? How will you practice your beliefs this year?

8.   How does faith support us in creating meaningful relationships or belonging? Where do you experience powerful community in your school? What are you investing in that community?

9.   How do the powerful concepts of forgiveness and acceptance flow from your faith?

10. It takes faith to dream. What is your dream for your life? What is your dream for your students, classroom, and school?

11. As you consider faith, describe any shifts you experience in your inner world.

Now reread your responses and highlight or underline any responses, words or phrases that deeply resonate. Create one Learn Forward action step.

WORTHINESS

Your thoughts are inspired. Write whatever comes to mind. Be as specific as possible.

1.   Describe when you feel a sense of dignity and worth. Name the students in your classroom who may be more desperate for that sense of dignity. How can you see them reaching out to get that need met? How can you proactively meet their need?

2.   My faith helps me understand the profound concepts of forgiveness and acceptance. Because of this understanding, I know my faith expands my sense of worthiness. What expands your sense of worthiness? What inspires you?

3.   How does your own sense of worthiness support you in reaching out to students and parents courageously?

4. What words does your heart need to hear? How can
    you share those messages with your students? How do
    those messages help students achieve their extraordinary
    potential?

5. Name one to five students who you feel are vulnerable in
    your classroom. What is unfinished for each of them? Write
    a one-sentence message of comfort to them. How can you
    creatively communicate that message to them?

6. Name a major achievement in your life. How did you make
    it? How did you overcome the obstacles? How did you
    continue forward under the pressure? How did you climb
    that mountain of pursuit? How can you share this story with
    your students this week?

7.   Describe your courageous ideal in handling the mistakes or
      failures of your students. Write down three practical ways
      you can infuse your classroom with the notion that "failure"
      is just a stone on a path to mastery?

8.   When we elevate process, over product, we offer children
      the opportunity to learn grit, tenacity, and perseverance.
      How can you 'cheer for the swing' in authentic ways in your
      classroom?

9.   Name one to five students you would like to offer something
      more to this week. What character traits are worthy in those
      students' hearts? How can you see those character traits
      manifesting in the students' lives? Try this as a practice with
      several students each week.

Now reread your responses and highlight or underline any responses, words or phrases that deeply resonate. Create one Learn Forward action step.

SELFHOOD

Your thoughts are inspired. Write whatever comes to mind. Be as specific as possible.

1. This year, how can you help your students set personalized learning goals in your classroom? How can you help them reflect on their progress towards those goals in a systematic way?

2. What students in your classroom are discovering their unique and special qualities? What students are struggling with that journey?

3. How can you support your students to dream about their lives in both the short and a bit longer term?

4. Which students are lacking in a sense of agency, initiative, or creativity? How can you create safety for their journey? How can you create connection with those students? How can you partner with parents to create a supportive plan?

5. What practices in your classroom demonstrate that you enjoy your students? What practices could you implement?

6. What do you need to thrive? List everything. Be specific. Why would modeling thriving be powerful? What would you need to change to become a better model?

7. If you are in survival mode, how can you take concrete steps this week, this month, and this year to move into a more grounded and stable place?

8. What are the signs one of your students is NOT thriving? Why aren't they thriving? What is your role in the journey? What isn't your role?

9. What does independence look like for your students? How can you effectively communicate with parents about your students' needs and growth towards independence? What powerful questions do you have about student independence?

10. In a class meeting or student conference, ask your students what support they might need from you to complete homework independently. Build routines you all agree upon in advance.

11. What systems do you need in place in your classroom to ensure you are holding your students accountable for independence, effort, and completion?

12. When do you feel most courageous? When do your students feel most courageous?

Now reread your responses and highlight or underline any responses, words or phrases that deeply resonate. Create one Learn Forward action step.

BELONGING

Your thoughts are inspired. Write whatever comes to mind. Be as specific as possible.

1. Belonging represents the journey of creating meaningful relationships. What are your most treasured relationships? Why?

2. Define your specific intentions to create a compassionate classroom community.

3. Classrooms and playgrounds are powerful spaces to practice creating community. How can we build empathy in students in those spaces?

4. How can we help students reflect on their experiences of community in those spaces and frame their experiences with courage and hopefulness?

5. How do you practice investing in your teaching team? Why? What do you have to give up or surrender? What do you gain?

6. How can you nurture acceptance and forgiveness in your students' hearts as they navigate friendship? How can you support students to cultivate a sense of personal boundaries and sense of self in friendships?

7. Parker Palmer writes about how hospitality is being with and welcoming someone different from oneself. How can you infuse your classroom experiences with a sense of hospitality?

8. What are the stories of courage in friendship worth telling in your classroom? What is an easy way of infusing a story-telling practice into your classroom?

9. How can you court your students into the safety of their learning community, as you inspire them to reach out towards others with a bright boldness to be in relationship?

10.   Belonging can happen in schools. How can you help someone feel like they belong today at school?

11.   Describe your schedule of class meetings. What is on your agenda for the next meeting?

Now reread your responses and highlight or underline any responses, words or phrases that deeply resonate. Create one Learn Forward action step.

CHANGEMAKING

Your thoughts are inspired. Write whatever comes to mind. Be as specific as possible.

1. "Make a conscious choice to be great." What is greatness? What is greatness in your classroom?

2. It takes courage to consider becoming a changemaking classroom. Where do you feel afraid? How can you move forward with the courage of a child?

3. What micro-changes do your students want in their classroom? Are they empowering?

4. Who embodies "bold love" as a changemaker in your family, community, or network?

5. What does it mean to you to 'hold the need you discover, unwaveringly?' Write a list of needs you have discovered in your learning community. Circle one or two you feel passionate about. How can you hold those needs as important over the next month? Over the next year?

6. How do you serve the 'greater good' even when your star doesn't shine? How do you move towards health and wholeness in a way that honours yourself and others?

7. What is the role of self-care and self-compassion in your life as you serve others?

8. Name the three most re-creating self-care strategies that actually release you further into changemaking.

9. What is sustainable change? What inspires you to take action to invest in sustainable change?

10. If vibrant teams lead change, how can you invest in the team around you?

11. Your learning community needs you! How can you support the creation of rich and meaningful experiences within your community?

12. What great and powerful ideas come to life in your students' eyes as you discuss the idea of becoming a changemaker with them?

Now reread your responses and highlight or underline any responses, words or phrases that deeply resonate. Create one Learn Forward practice that you can implement this week to help you focus on what matters most.

What happened? We would love to hear your story. Just use *#LFstories* to share on your social media channels or blog.

For more information about Learn Forward programs for educators and schools visit www.learnforward.ca

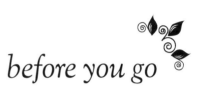

before you go

At the Table of Learning our powerful partnerships with teachers, parents, and children will co-create an organic and rich learning journey. It will be a learning journey for all of us. We will all change from the inside out.

We need soft hearts. Our soft hearts will ready us to engage in the most powerful experience on the planet: supporting another human being's growth and development. I believe every caregiver, parent, and teacher wishes for the best for their children. Embracing our vulnerability with courage will help us remain in a soft place of learning.

Our soft hearts, however, are not intended in place of high expectations. 'Soft hearts' does not mean indulgent, permissive, or laissez-faire. We are parenting and teaching our children to be independent! It is heroic work.

Let's all wear high expectations for our children like a badge, a badge of courage. We must courageously determine each day to focus on what matters.

What we knit into the daily lives of children is the only way to realize high expectations. But, there isn't one colour of yarn. It is a creative and dynamic process.

Holding and believing in the extraordinary potential living within every child takes tremendous courage.

So, with soft hearts and heroic courage, Learn Forward is our invitation to focus on what really matters:

faith,
worthiness,
selfhood,
belonging,
and changemaking.

We need all of the journeys. They work in concert. The symphony of experience provides insight into the next right thing.

We need each other to Learn Forward.

As teachers and parents, our sacred work lives in the paradox of daily routines along with the breadth of our experiences with the five journeys. It is both. We need to step sure-footed each day guided by our good instincts and use the journeys to discover over time how to bring rich goodness to the life of a child.

So, whether you are raising little birds in your home nest or have a classroom full, I hope Learn Forward liberates you to be on the organic, rewarding, and most important journeys.

I wish for the courage to deepen the connections and enjoy our children.

For the sake of the children,
Learn Forward.

notes

INTRODUCTION

Brené Brown, *The Gifts of Imperfection*, (Center City: Hazelden, 2010).

PART ONE
STORIES OF COURAGE

CHAPTER 3

Margaret Wheatley, *Turning to One Another: Simple Conversations to Restore Hope to the Future, Expanded Second Edition* (San Francisco: Bennett-Koehler, 2009).

PART TWO
THE PATH TO LEARN FORWARD

CHAPTER 4

Mark Nepo, *Understory* (poem), *theteachermanifesto.wordpress.com* (blog post), November 26, 2014, theteachermanifesto.wordpress.com/2014/11/

CHAPTER 5

Parker Palmer, *Let Your Life Speak: Listening for the Voice of Vocation*, (San Francisco: Jossey-Bass, 2000).

Ethel Kessler, Leonard Kessler, *Stan the Hot Dog Man*, (New York: Harper Collins, 1990).

Omid Safi, "You're Not Any Cooler than Jesus or Muhammad," onbeing.org (blog), April 2, 2015, onbeing.org/blog/youre-not-any-cooler-than-jesus-or-muhammad/7447 (accessed April 4, 2015).

PART THREE
THE FIVE JOURNEYS

CHAPTER 6 FAITH

Mark Nepo, *The Endless Practice: Becoming Who You Were Born to Be*, (New York: Simon & Schuster, 2014).

Natalie Grant, "When I Leave the Room," *Hurricane*, 2013, Curb Records.

Charles Duhigg, *The Power of Habit: Why We Do What We Do in Life and Business*, (Toronto: Doubleday Canada, 2012).

CHAPTER 7 WORTHINESS

E. E. Cummings, "Quote," brainyquote.com (website), brainyquote.com/quotes/quotes/e/eecummin389141.html (accessed August 4, 2015).

Laura Hillenbrand, *Unbroken: A World War II Story of Survival, Resilience, and Redemption*, (New York: Random House, 2010).

Brené Brown, *The Gifts of Imperfection*, (Center City, MN: Hazelden, 2010).

Keith Urban, "Kiss the Girl", *Defying Gravity*, 2009, Capitol Records Nashville.

Parker Palmer, *Let Your Life Speak: Listening for the Voice of Vocation*, (San Francisco: Jossey-Bass, 2000).

CHAPTER 8 SELFHOOD

Richard Rohr, "God Creates Things That Create Themselves," stjohnsquamish.ca, (blog), stjohnsquamish.ca/richard-rohr-god-creates-things-that-create-themselves/ (accessed 2015).

Willowstone Academy, "Willowstone Academy Manifesto," willowstoneacademy.com, (PDF & video), June 20, 2014, willowstoneacademy.com/about/our-manifesto/ (accessed 2015).

Dr. Seuss, "5 Lessons from Dr. Seuss", Infographic, taniamccartney.blogspot.ca, (blog), July 23, 2012, taniamccartney.blogspot.ca/2012/07/5-lessons-from-dr-seuss.html (accessed 2015).

Dr. Gordon Neufeld, Gabor Maté, *Hold On to Your Kids: Why Parents Need to Matter More Than Peers*, (Toronto: Penguin Random House Canada, 2013).

Richard Rohr, "Living Life in a Straight Line," Soulstream.org (blog), August 25, 2014, soulstream.org/living-life-straight-line/ (accessed 2015).

Sabre Cherkowski, *"What if we imagine..."* (PowerPoint slides). Retrieved from Summer Series Lecture, Summer Institute in Education Speaker Series, UBC-O, August, 2014.

Erwin Raphael McManus, *The Artisan Soul: Crafting Your Life into a Work of Art*, (New York: Harper Collins, 2014).

M. Scott Peck, "Quote," brainyquote.com (website), http://www.brainyquote.com/quotes/quotes/m/mscottpec392902.html, (accessed May 3, 2015).

CHAPTER 10 BELONGING

Brené Brown. *The Gifts of Imperfection*, (Center City: Hazelden, 2010).

Daniel Goleman, *Emotional Intelligence: Why It Can Matter More Than IQ*, (New York: Random House, 1995).

Carolyn Gregoire, "The 75 Year Study That Found the Secrets to a Fulfilling Life," huffingtonpost.com (blog), August 11, 2013, huffingtonpost.com/2013/08/11/how-this-harvard-psycholo_n_3727229.html (accessed 2015).

Willowstone Academy, "Willowstone Academy Manifesto," willowstoneacademy.com, (PDF & video), June 20, 2014, willowstoneacademy.com/about/our-manifesto/ (accessed 2015).

Anne MacLean. "UBCO Practicum Placement Request", Message to the author. August 18, 2014. Email.

Jane Nelsen, Lynn Lott, and H. Stephen Glenn, *Positive Discipline in the Classroom*, (Rocklin: Prima Publishing, 1993).

CHAPTER 11 CHANGEMAKING

"Be Great" video by Luck Companies. https://vimeo.
com/29780708, Virginia, Produced by Luck Companies, 2011.

I John 3:18 NIV.

Victoria Safford, "On Hope", a poem, onbeing.org (podcast).
January 8, 2015, "The Inner Life of Rebellion", http://www.
onbeing.org/program/parker-palmer-and-courtney-martin-the-
inner-life-of-rebellion/7122 (accessed March 1, 2015).

Willowstone Academy, "Willowstone Academy Manifesto,"
willowstoneacademy.com, (PDF & video), June 20, 2014,
willowstoneacademy.com/about/our-manifesto/ (accessed 2015).

PART FOUR
THE TABLE OF LEARNING

CHAPTER 12 A LEARNING COMMUNITY IS LIKE BEING AT A TABLE

Henry Ford, "Quote," brainyquote.com (website), www.
brainyquote.com/quotes/quotes/h/henryford121997.html
(accessed April 24, 2015).

Parker Palmer, *The Courage to Teach: Exploring the Inner Landscape of a Teacher's Life*, (San Francisco: Jossey-Bass, 1998).

acknowledgements

For me, everything is grace. The opportunity to write my story and thoughts is yet another great grace. While I wrote alone, it is a community bringing forth Learn Forward! The mystery of messy togetherness is weaving the tapestry of Learn Forward.

I am ever-grateful for...

Our team of vibrant educators at Willowstone Academy. Each day you pour out your life, energy, and creativity for the sake of the children. It is a picture of heavenly goodness that calls me to be better. It is my honor to serve with you!

Heather Sandager. You are the perfect balance of being both led and leading us to Learn Forward! I appreciate your beauty in my world.

Sherry Parker. Thank you for being there for the under-dog, especially when that's me. You are a genius for details and insight into children's hearts.

Jessica Krebs. You faithfully create, systematize, organize, capture, and order my world. The breadth of your service is as wide as the sea. Each year gets better and after a decade it measures on the "tremendous" scale!

Willowstone Academy families. It is a privilege to watch your children learn and grow. Creating a learning community together is a wonderful adventure of Learn Forward proportions.

Sam Turya. Your leadership and loyalty make change. Thank you for believing in Niteo right from the start and giving generously of your time, attention, and oversight for the sake of the children of the world! I learn so much from you.

Michelle Davies. You took my soul and designed a digital space.

Roselyn Minnes. Your artistry began with an ink pen, and your creativity gave our tree and Learn Forward life, beauty, and dignity. It moves me.

Our first nest-building families. On a couple of Friday nights in spring, The Builder and I found a garden of learning. We didn't just share our "visioning weekend," we called you friends.

Jimmy and Lindsay Troge. Your friendship and faithfulness teach me about what matters most. I am ever-grateful for the time and timelessness of our relationship. We can't wait until the next time when we will meet again. Thank you, Lindsay, for serving as the Copy Editor for Learn Forward.

Miranda Webb. You spent hours with me cultivating the soil of my story, tilling it until it broke open to give life. Then, you planted and tended Learn Forward with me. Learn Forward would not exist without your hunger to be fed from its garden. It is my privilege to be on this sacred journey with you, as professionals and mothers. Thank you for serving as the Editor for Learn Forward.

My brothers, Lance, and Lane. Your leadership, service, and dear ones bring joy to my family and me.

My sister, Renee. No one has seen more of me! No one has championed me more over the course of my lifetime. No one has so loyally walked through the valley of the shadow of death with me. Learn Forward began upstairs on Monroe Way and was watered with many of my tears throughout the days of our lives. Thank you for being there. Thank you for loving my family generously. I love you and yours.

My Mom and Dad. Learn Forward is primarily your wisdom written down. It is my tree of life. You are the most wonderful parents and grandparents the world could ever find!

My dearest ones, Daniel Liegmann, Alyssa Liegmann, and Gracyn Dawn Veldhoen. Your courage is woven into each and every page of this book. Thank you for linking arms with me to send out our story in service of the greater good. I am in constant awe of my pure privilege of calling you my own. I am never happier than with our family-of-five. Amazing grace.

The Builder. Loving you is easy. Finding you each morning and at day's end is my abundant life. Our love makes my world spin. Your gifts, strengths, and provision bless our children and the children of the world. Thank you for being willing to Learn Forward with me!

To the Greater Mystery. Across the globe and from our depths, we cry out to be rooted in faith, hope, and love.

Focused on what truly matters.

For the sake of the children,

Karine

about the author

Karine Veldhoen, M.Ed., is the founder of Learn Forward and a creative force in education. She's also the Chief Learning Officer at Willowstone Academy, the CEO/Founder of Niteo Africa, a former Education Consultant for FreshGrade and a modern day pilgrim.

Learn Forward™ represents a lifetime of personal experience, professional study, action research, and meaning-making within the context of education.

She's been exploring the most important journeys of children through serving as the Chief Learning Officer at Willowstone Academy for the last ten years and as an educator for over two decades. Learn Forward is a culmination of her work with thousands of children and their families in two states, two provinces, and around the globe.

She writes and speaks about co-designing a more organic educational path for children. In her talks about the transformation of education, she emphasizes the importance of cultivating a connection between school and home. She uses the Table of Learning as a metaphor for where we can begin to co-create the conditions for children to thrive.

When she's not carving new paths in education, you'll find her at the lake with a good book. After 20 years in the United States, she now lives with her husband and three children, her heart-song in the Okanagan Valley, British Columbia.

CONNECT WITH KARINE

Blog: learnforward.ca/blog
Twitter: twitter.com/Mrs_KV
Facebook: facebook.com/karine.veldhoen

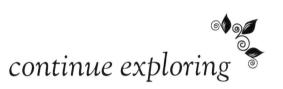

continue exploring

To continue exploring and get the latest Learn Forward resources, visit:

www.learnforward.ca

This book is available for bulk sale. To inquire about purchasing ten or more copies at pricing packaged to share, please send a note to hello@learnforward.ca.

To get a free digital copy of the Learn Forward Starter Kit and subscribe to my blog, visit www.learnforward.ca/starterkit.

THE
#LEARNFORWARD
APP

AVAILABLE FOR IOS AND ANDROID

FOCUS ON WHAT MATTERS MOST.
DEEPEN YOUR CONNECTION.
ENJOY YOUR CHILD MORE.

Get inspiring messages delivered to
your handheld device to remind you
about what matters most.

LEARNFORWARD.CA/SHOP

LEARN FORWARD
PROGRAMS
FOR PARENTS AND EDUCATORS

Cultivate the conditions for thriving
at home and at school.

NEST-BUILDING COURSES & RETREAT FOR PARENTS

Design a home life where connections thrive.

LEARN FORWARD PRIVATE WORKSHOP FOR SCHOOLS

Meaning-making and culture-building to
engage and inspire your community.

LEARN FORWARD COACHING FOR PARENTS & EDUCATORS

Nurture your sacred work and create a more
organic educational path.

LEARNFORWARD.CA